Rick Steves

POCKET

ITALY'S
CINQUE TERRE

Rick Steves

Contents

Introduction

Tucked between Genoa and Pisa, in a mountainous and seductive corner of the Italian Riviera, lies the Cinque Terre (CHINK-weh TAY-reh)—five villages carving a good life out of difficult terrain. With a traffic-free charm—a happy result of natural isolation—the Cinque Terre offers a rugged alternative to the beachy Riviera resorts nearby.

Each village fills a ravine with a lazy hive of human activity. There isn't a Fiat or museum in sight—just sun, sea, sand (well, pebbles), and wine. Choose a home base according to just how cut off you'd like to be from the outer world: resorty Monterosso, cover-girl Vernazza, hilltop Corniglia, photogenic Manarola, or amiable Riomaggiore.

The Cinque Terre at a Glance

The Cinque Terre

▲**Monterosso al Mare** Resorty, relatively level, and spread out along the coast, with a charming old town, a modern new town, and the Cinque Terre's best beaches, swimming, and nightlife. It has the most restaurants and the most comfortable hotels. See page 33.

▲▲▲**Vernazza** The region's gem, dramatically crowned with a ruined castle above and a lively harborfront cradling a natural harbor below. See page 55.

▲**Corniglia** Quiet hilltop village known for its cooler temperatures (it's the only one without a harbor), fewer tourists, and a tradition of fine wines. See page 81.

▲▲**Manarola** Hiking-focused waterfront village wrapped in vineyards and dotted with a picturesque mix of shops and cliff-climbing houses. See page 89.

▲▲**Riomaggiore** The most workaday of the five villages—with night-life, too. See page 103.

Near the Cinque Terre

▲**Levanto** Town popular with surfers and families for its long beach; just one stop by train from the Cinque Terre. It offers an easy, level hike (or bike ride) to the sleepy villages of Bonassola and Framura. See page 119.

▲**Sestri Levante** Charming town on a peninsula flanked by two crescent beaches. See page 131.

▲▲**Santa Margherita Ligure** Easygoing old-school resort town with just enough urban bustle, a handful of sights, and proximity to Portofino. See page 137.

▲**Portofino** Yacht-harbor resort with grand scenery, an easy hop (by boat, bus, or on foot) from Santa Margherita Ligure. See page 149.

▲▲**Porto Venere** Enchanting seafront village perfect for a scenic day trip (by boat or bus). See page 155.

La Spezia Beachless transportation hub, with trains and boats to the Cinque Terre and buses and boats to Porto Venere. See page 160.

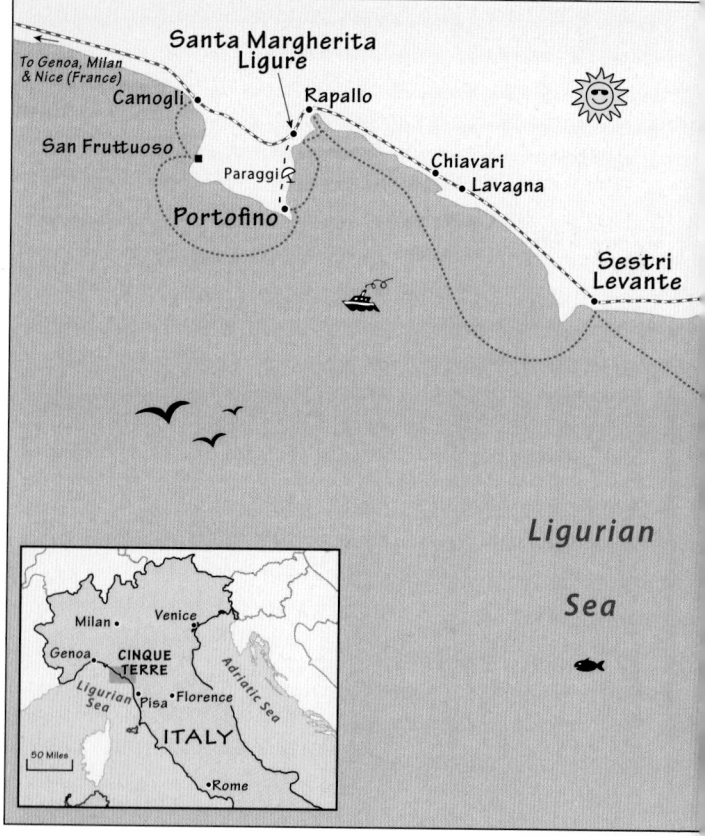

About This Book

Rick Steves Pocket Cinque Terre is a personal tour guide...in your pocket. The core of the book is six chapters that zero in on each of the Cinque Terre's five towns (plus one for nearby destinations), highlighting the region's greatest sights and experiences. The Monterosso al Mare chapter takes you through the old and new sections of the

Cinque Terre Area Public Transport

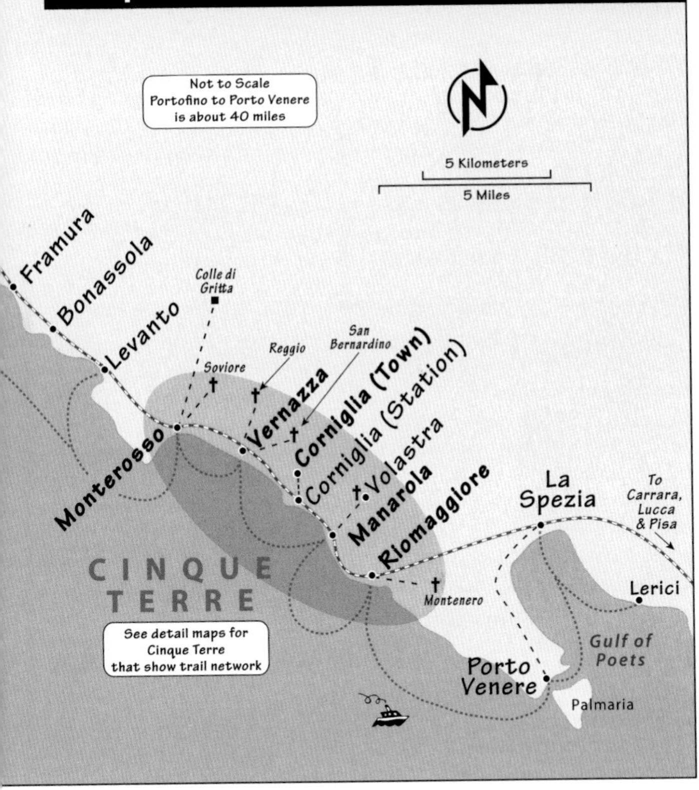

Not to Scale
Portofino to Porto Venere
is about 40 miles

N

5 Kilometers

5 Miles

Framura
Bonassola
Colle di Gritta
Levanto
Soviore
Reggio
San Bernardino
Vernazza
Corniglia (Town)
Corniglia (Station)
Monterosso
Volastra
Manarola
Riomaggiore
La Spezia
To Carrara, Lucca & Pisa

CINQUE TERRE

Montenero

Lerici

See detail maps for
Cinque Terre
that show trail network

Gulf of Poets

Porto Venere

Palmaria

Cinque Terre's liveliest town, with the most restaurants and best beaches. The Vernazza chapter introduces you to the jewel of the five towns, with its picturesque harbor and pastel canyon of homes. You'll also get to know the sleepy, mellow, and laid-back villages of Corniglia, Manarola, and Riomaggiore, along with nearby beach towns and functional villages a short train or boat ride away.

The rest of this book is a traveler's tool kit, with my best advice on how to save money, plan your time, and use public transportation. You'll also get recommendations on hotels, restaurants, and activities.

Planning Your Time

The following day plans give you an idea of how much an organized, motivated, and caffeinated person can see. The ideal stay in the Cinque Terre is two or three full days; at the least, give yourself two nights and an uninterrupted day.

The villages are connected by trains, boats, and trails. There's no checklist of sights or experiences—just a hike, the towns themselves, and your fondest vacation desires. Read this chapter in advance to piece together your best visit, mixing hiking, swimming, trains, and boat rides.

Cinque Terre in Two Days: You could spend one day hiking between towns (taking a boat or train part of the way, or as the return trip). Spend a second day visiting any towns you've yet to see, comparing main streets, beaches, and focaccia.

Here's a sample day: If you're based in Monterosso, take a morning train to Corniglia, hike to Vernazza for lunch (where you could explore the town, hike to the grand view cemetery, or cool off at the beach), then catch the boat back to Monterosso to stroll the beach promenade. And that's only one day out of dozens of memorable Cinque Terre combinations you can dream up.

On any evening, linger over dinner, enjoy live music at a low-key club (or opera singers in Vernazza), try a wine tasting, or follow one of my self-guided town walks. At sunset, take a glass of your favorite beverage out to the breakwater to watch the sun slip into the Mediterranean.

With More Time: Frequent trains make day trips along the coast easy (though seeing Portofino is more relaxed if you overnight in Santa Margherita Ligure). A day trip to Levanto is a snap (by train, boat, or a hike from Monterosso) and a side excursion from Levanto to Bonassola and Framura is fun. For double the beaches, visit Sestri Levante. South of the Cinque Terre, reach lovely Porto Venere by boat, or by train and bus via La Spezia.

Day-Tripping to the Cinque Terre: Speed demons could store their baggage, take a hike in the morning, have a waterfront lunch, laze on a beach in the afternoon, and leave by evening to somewhere back in the

Rick's Free Video Clips and Audio Tours

Rick Steves Classroom Europe, a powerful tool for teachers, is also useful for travelers. This video library contains about 500 short clips excerpted from my public television series. Enjoy these videos as you sort through options for your trip and to better understand what you'll see in Europe. Check it out at Classroom.RickSteves.com (just enter a topic to find everything I've filmed on a subject).

Rick Steves Audio Europe, a free app, makes it easy to download my audio tours and listen to them offline as you travel. The app also offers interviews (organized by country) from my public radio show with experts from Europe and around the globe. Find it in your app store or at RickSteves.com/AudioEurope.

real world. But be warned: The Cinque Terre is inundated with cruise-ship groups doing the same thing. The best way to enjoy the Cinque Terre is to be here before and after the daily day-trip deluge. (Ironically, some travelers decide against an overnight because they've heard the Cinque Terre is crowded—then day-trip in, only experiencing it with those terrible crowds.) The charm of the region survives—early and late.

When to Go

May, June, September, and early October are ideal times (though May is a popular time for tour groups), with more pleasant hiking weather and lower prices than the local vacation months of July and August. If you do come in July or August, book further ahead, and get up early to enjoy the trails before the heat of the day—perhaps even before breakfast. April weekends can be very busy: Easter and the public holidays of Liberation Day (April 25) and Labor Day (May 1) bring crowds of Italians, prices shoot up, and restaurants fill. Weekdays are quieter at any time of year.

Flexible and open-minded travelers can enjoy a trip in March or late October, perhaps even late February or early November, but should plan for chilly weather, fewer or no boats, and shuttered shops, restaurants, and hotels (many close from November to mid-March). The midwinter months are really dead.

Make time in the Cinque Terre to wander, eat gelato, and simply be.

Before You Go

You'll have a smoother trip if you tackle a few things ahead of time. For more details on these topics, see the Practicalities chapter and RickSteves.com, which has helpful travel-tip articles and videos.

Make sure your travel documents are valid. If your passport is due to expire within six months of your ticketed date of return, you need to renew it. Allow six weeks or more to renew or get a passport (www.travel.state.gov). Check for current Covid entry requirements, such as proof of vaccination or a negative Covid-19 test result.

Arrange your transportation. Book your international flights. Figure out your transportation options. If traveling beyond the Cinque Terre, research train reservations, rail passes, and car rentals. Drivers: Consider bringing an International Driving Permit (sold at AAA offices in the US, www.aaa.com) along with your license.

Book rooms well in advance, especially if your trip falls during peak season or any major holidays or festivals.

Consider travel insurance. Compare the cost of insurance to the cost of your potential loss. Check whether your existing insurance (health, homeowners, or renters) covers you and your possessions overseas.

Call your bank. Alert your bank that you'll be using your debit and credit cards in Europe. Ask about transaction fees, and, if you don't already have one, get a "contactless" credit card (request your card PIN, too). You don't need to bring euros; you can withdraw euros from cash machines in Europe.

Use your smartphone smartly. Sign up for an international service plan to reduce your costs, or rely on Wi-Fi in Europe instead. Download any apps you'll want on the road, such as maps, translators, transit schedules, and Rick Steves Audio Europe (see sidebar, earlier).

Pack light. You'll walk with your luggage more than you think. I travel for weeks with a single carry-on bag and a day pack. Use the packing checklist in Practicalities as a guide.

Travel Smart

If you have a positive attitude, equip yourself with good information (this book), and expect to travel smart, you will.

Pickpockets abound in crowded places where tourists congregate. Treat commotions as smokescreens for theft. Keep your cash, credit cards, and passport secure in a money belt tucked under your clothes; carry only a day's spending money in your front pocket or wallet.

If you wilt easily, choose a hotel with air-conditioning, start your day early, take a midday siesta, and resume your sightseeing later.

Be sure to schedule in slack time for picnics, laundry, people-watching, leisurely dinners, shopping, and recharging your touristic batteries. Slow down and be open to unexpected experiences and the hospitality of the Italian people.

Sample *antipasti* with a glass of wine as the Mediterranean shimmers before you, take in the Riviera's rugged coastline from a lazy boat ride, or hike a trail to get a bird's-eye view of the region's colorful villages. As you visit places I know and love, I'm happy you'll be meeting some of my favorite Italians.

Happy travels! *Buon viaggio!*

The Cinque Terre

This breathtakingly scenic six-mile stretch of coast was first described in medieval times as the "five lands" (*cinque terre*). Tiny communities grew up in the shadows of castles, which doubled as lookouts for pirate raids. As the threat of pirates faded, the villages prospered, catching fish and cultivating grapes. Until the advent of tourism, the towns—Monterosso, Vernazza, Corniglia, Manarola, and Riomaggiore—remained isolated. Even today, each village comes with its own traditions, a distinct dialect, and a proud heritage. Other Italians think of locals here as "mountain people by the sea."

ORIENTATION TO THE CINQUE TERRE

The Cinque Terre is now a national park (founded in 1999), where all can enjoy the villages, hiking, swimming, boat rides, and evening romance of one of God's great gifts to tourism. While the region is well discovered and can get jam-packed, I've never seen happier, more relaxed tourists.

This chapter focuses on how to navigate the Cinque Terre, using a mix of trains, boats, and hikes. Chapters on each town follow, with all the specifics you need for your visit. For general advice on travel in Italy, see the Practicalities chapter.

Tourist and Park Information

Each town's train station has a Cinque Terre national park information office, which doubles as an all-purpose town TI and gift shop. They can answer questions about trails (including conditions and closures), shuttle bus schedules, and so on. You can also call the park's main phone number (+39 0187 762 600) or visit their useful website, ParcoNazionale5terre.it.

A blog worth a look is CinqueTerreInsider.com, written by resident American expat Amy Inman; it's filled with practicalities for visitors to this always-in-flux region.

Arrival in the Cinque Terre

By Train: The five towns of the Cinque Terre are on a milk-run line, with trains coming through about twice an hour on their way between La Spezia and points north. Fast long-distance trains usually speed right through the Cinque Terre without stopping, although a few serve Monterosso and let you get there directly from Milan or Pisa. Otherwise, expect to connect to a local train at La Spezia's Centrale station (if coming from the south) or at Genoa, Sestri Levante, or Levanto (from the north).

For details on riding the train between Cinque Terre towns, see "Getting Around the Cinque Terre," later in this chapter; for information on arrival in each town, see the "Arrival" section in each town chapter. For outbound trains, see "Monterosso Connections" on page 53 and "La Spezia Connections" on page 163.

By Car (Not Recommended): Don't bring a car to the Cinque Terre; you won't need it. Given the narrow roads and parking headaches, the only Cinque Terre town I'd drive to is Monterosso (and only if my hotel had parking). Park your car in a larger town nearby and take the train

The Cinque Terre

in: It's safer, cheaper, faster, and smarter. Parking is easy in Levanto or La Spezia (La Spezia has a fine modern underground garage at the station). A rare exception is if you're lodging in the hills above one of the Cinque Terre towns, in which case driving might be less hassle than lugging bags up from a train station (ask your hotelier for advice).

Helpful Hints

Pickpocket Alert: At peak times, the Cinque Terre can be notoriously crowded, and pickpockets (often teens in groups of three or four, frequently dressed as tourists) aggressively and expertly work the most congested areas. Be on guard, especially in train stations, on platforms, and while you're on trains, particularly when getting on or off with a crush of people. Wear a money belt, and keep your things zipped up and buttoned down.

Money: You'll find ATMs and banks throughout the region. Use ATMs attached to actual banks. Shops earn a commission by hosting rip-off ATMs on their premises.

Markets: Market days perk up the Cinque Terre and nearby towns from around 8:00 to 13:00 on Tuesday in Vernazza, Wednesday in Levanto, Thursday in Monterosso, Friday in Santa Margherita Ligure, and Saturday in Sestri Levante.

Booking Services: Arbaspàa, based in Manarola, sets up wine tastings, cooking classes, fishing trips, and more (www.arbaspaa.com; see page 98). **Cinque Terre Riviera,** based in Vernazza, books rooms and apartments throughout the region, Vernazza opera tickets, cooking classes, and more (www.cinqueterreriviera.com; see page 57). **BeautifuLiguria,** run by Anna Merulla, offers various excursions (www.beautifuliguria.com).

Local Guides: Two knowledgeable guides, both a delight to be with, are **Andrea Bordigoni** (€130/half-day, €230/day, +39 393 133 9409, bordigo@inwind.it) and **Marco Brizzi** (€125/half-day, €210/day, +39 328 694 2847, marco_brizzi@yahoo.it).

Baggage Storage and Delivery: You can pay to store bags at or near the train stations in Monterosso and Riomaggiore. Near the Cinque Terre, you can store bags in Santa Margherita Ligure and in La Spezia. To transfer luggage from the station to your accommodations, call ahead and arrange with **Roberto Pecunia;** he's based in Riomaggiore but works in any of the towns (+39 370 375 7972, www.robytransport5terre.com).

Taxi: These traffic-free towns are set up for train access, but there are a few cases, like group airport transfers, where a taxi makes sense. **Cinqueterre Taxi,** based in Levanto, covers all five towns (Matteo +39 334 776 1946, Christian +39 347 652 0837, www.cinqueterretaxi.com). The pricey **5 Terre Transfer** is in Riomaggiore (Luciana +39 339 130 1183, Marzio +39 340 356 5268, www.5terretransfer.com).

Getting Around the Cinque Terre

Trains are the cheapest, fastest, and most frequent way to connect towns within the Cinque Terre. But don't get stuck in a train rut: In calm weather, boats connect the towns nearly as frequently—and with much better scenery.

By Train

The five towns are just a few minutes apart by train.

Tickets: A train ride between any two Cinque Terre towns costs €5—steep for such a short trip, as the price includes a park fee (from November to March there's no fee and tickets cost €2.10). You *must* buy a new **individual ticket** for every train ride. You can buy tickets online or with the Trenitalia app (www.trenitalia.com), at ticket machines (at each station), at Cinque Terre park desks, or at staffed ticket windows in Monterosso, Levanto, and La Spezia. Don't wait to buy a ticket at the last minute: Ticket machines can be broken, and there can be very long lines at the window.

The Cinque Terre **Treno Card** (€18.20/day, described later, under "Hiking the Cinque Terre") can be worthwhile even if you don't hike, as it allows you to catch trains at the last minute without ticket concerns. It pays for itself if you take four rides in one day, but its value comes more from convenience than economy (https://card.parconazionale5terre.it).

Trains are covered by the Eurail Pass, but it doesn't make sense to use up a valuable travel day here.

Using Tickets and Cards: Your ticket (or park card) must be validated before you board (though many are prevalidated and you don't need to do anything). This includes tickets bought online or with the Trenitalia app, and tickets that list a specific train time. Other tickets and passes are "open," and you must validate them by stamping them in one of the green-and-white machines located on train platforms and in station passages. Conductors here are notorious for levying stiff fines on tourists riding with an unstamped ticket. Red-vested trackside staff can answer your train-related questions.

Schedules: In peak season, trains connecting the five towns generally run two to three times hourly in each direction, but the frequency declines after about 20:00. Shops, hotels, and restaurants often post the current schedule, and many hand out paper copies. Study the key to know which departures are only for weekdays, Sundays, and so on. Make a note of the departure time of the train you want to take and ideally its train number and final destination, as that's how the station monitors identify departing trains.

Printed schedules also tell you which towns any given train

will stop in. Some trains skip lesser stations (particularly Vernazza, Corniglia, and Manarola).

At the Station: Look for monitors that display upcoming departures, listed by time, train number, and final destination (they do not show intermediate stops). They also show if a train is late—*in ritardo*—and by how many minutes—*SOPP* means "cancelled." Note your platform number (*binario*). On the platform, digital displays reconfirm the train's final destination and usually show a list of intermediate stops. Confirm that the train will stop where you want on this display, or check the yellow "Partenze" posters.

Northbound trains (using the tracks closest to the water) are going to Levanto, Sestri Levante, or Genova; southbound trains (using tracks on the mountain side) are headed for La Spezia.

Getting Off: As the train leaves the town previous to your destination, go to the door and get ready to slip out before the mobs flood in at your stop. Note that stations are small and trains are long—you might have to get off deep in a tunnel, especially in Vernazza and Riomaggiore (just head toward daylight). Train doors don't open automatically—you may have to push the green button, twist the black handle, or lift up the red one.

By Boat

From late March through October, a daily boat service connects Monterosso, Vernazza, Manarola, Riomaggiore, Porto Venere, and beyond. Though they can be very crowded, these boats provide a scenic way to get from town to town (operated by Consorzio 5 Terre Golfo dei Poeti, +39 0187 732 987, www.navigazionegolfodeipoeti.it).

Because the boats nose in and tourists disembark over little more than a plank, even just a small chop can cancel some or all stops.

Trains connect the towns.

Many Cinque Terre streets are car-free.

Swimming and Kayaking

Every coastal town has a beach—or, at least, a rocky place to **swim.** Monterosso has the Cinque Terre's biggest and sandiest beach, with umbrellas and beach-use fees (but any stretch of beach without umbrellas is free). Vernazza's main beach and new beach are tiny—better for sunning than swimming (some people swim in the deep water off the breakwater). Manarola and Riomaggiore have the worst beaches (no sand), but Manarola offers the best deep-water swimming. Levanto, just a few minutes' train ride past Monterosso, has big, broad beaches, with even

better ones an easy bike ride away, in Bonassola and Framura. And Sestri Levante, farther north, has two beautiful beaches.

Several beaches have showers. Don't tote your white hotel towels; most hotels will provide beach towels (sometimes for a fee). Underwater sightseeing is full of fish. Sea urchins line the rocks, and sometimes jellyfish wash up on the pebbles (water shoes and goggles sold in local shops). If no one is swimming, it's likely because of stinging jellyfish. Ask, *"Medusa?"*

You can rent **kayaks** or **boats** in Monterosso and Riomaggiore. While experienced boaters have a blast here, if you're not comfortable navigating a tippy kayak, this is not a good place to learn.

Tickets: Ticket prices depend on the length of the boat ride (€7 for a short hop; up to €20 for a five-town, one-way ride with stops). An all-day Cinque Terre pass costs €30; if you add Porto Venere, it's €37, plus an optional €5 extra for a 40-minute scenic ride around three small islands near Porto Venere (2/day). Buy tickets at the little stands at each town's harbor.

Schedules: Boat schedules are posted online and at docks, harbor

Crowd-Beating Tips

Italy's slice of traffic-free Riviera has been discovered, frustrating both locals and conscientious visitors. The most dramatic influx is created by groups—both day-tripping tours and mobs of cruise-ship sightseers. Avoid the worst of the logjams by following these tips:

Time your visit. July, August, and spring holiday weekends (Easter, Liberation Day on April 25, and Labor Day on May 1) are the busiest times of the year. Weekends are more crowded than week-days. Late spring (aside from holidays) and early fall generally have fewer crowds and cooler temperatures for hiking (although it can be too cold to swim).

Make the most of early and late hours. Take advantage of the cool, relaxed, and quiet mornings and evenings. Starting a hike at 8:00 or at 16:00 or 17:00 is a joy; dining after 18:00 is a delight. Cruisers and day-trippers start pouring into the Cinque Terre around 10:00 and typically head out by 17:00. Those midday hours are your time to hit the beach or find a hike away from the main trails. At midday, the main coastal trail is a hot human traffic jam. Beyond the busy coastal trail, there are plenty of hikes where you'll scarcely see another tourist.

Sleep in the Cinque Terre—not nearby. Levanto and La Spezia are close and well connected by train, making them popular home bases. But it's easier to enjoy the Cinque Terre early and late—when it's quiet and cool—if you're sleeping here.

Be careful on crowded train platforms. At peak times, be cautious, stay well behind the yellow line, and be alert for pickpockets. Spread out to less crowded areas to wait.

Hire your own boat. If regularly scheduled boats are jammed, consider hiring your own boat to zip you to the next town. Captains hang out at each town's harbor, offering one-way transfers to other towns, hour-long cruises, and more.

bars, Cinque Terre park offices, and hotels. Boats depart Monterosso about hourly (9:30-17:00), stopping at the Cinque Terre towns (except Corniglia, the hill town) and ending up about 90 minutes later in Porto Venere. In the other direction, boats depart Porto Venere toward Monterosso about hourly (8:30-17:00). In high season, a few boats per day extend the route from Monterosso north to Levanto, and from Porto Venere east to La Spezia.

Private Boats: To escape the crowds—or for a scenic splurge—hire a captain to ferry you between towns. For example, at the harbor in Vernazza, you can pay around €50 to hop to any other Cinque Terre town. Split the cost among a few fellow travelers, and you have an affordable water taxi. See the specific listing in each town.

By Shuttle Bus

ATC shuttle buses, which locals call *pulmino*, connect each Cinque Terre town with its closest parking lot and various points in the hills (but they don't connect the five towns to each other). The one you're most likely to use runs between Corniglia's train station and its hilltop town center. Rides cost €1.50 (€2.50 from driver) and are covered by the Cinque Terre park card (described in next section). Buy tickets and get bus schedules at park info offices or TIs, or check times posted at bus stops (also online at www.atcesercizio.it). As you board, it's smart to tell the driver where you want to go. Departures often coordinate with train arrival times.

Some shuttles go beyond the parking lots and high into the hills, often terminating at the town's sanctuary church. To soak in the scenery, you can ride up and hike down. This works particularly well from Manarola and Vernazza. Or you can ride both ways (50 minutes round-trip, covered by one ticket).

Boats connect the towns.

Shuttles link to parking and hikes.

HIKING THE CINQUE TERRE

The five Cinque Terre towns are connected directly by a main coastal trail, and indirectly by a web of trails higher up. Unfortunately, the two southern sections of the main coastal trail have been closed for the last few years due to falling rocks (Corniglia to Manarola, and Manarola to Riomaggiore). The two longer, northern sections remain open (Monterosso to Vernazza and Vernazza to Corniglia).

With so many day-trippers blitzing in with the same hiking agenda, go early or late if you want to enjoy either of the open coastal sections. At any time of day, consider the paths that run higher up and farther inland. They are less crowded, free to use, and just as scenic. The single best high-country hike is from Manarola to Corniglia via Volastra.

Cinque Terre Park Cards: Visitors hiking on the main coastal trail must buy a park card. Cards are not needed to hike on higher trails. Cards can be purchased online, or at train stations, TIs, and trailheads (http://card.parconazionale5terre.it). Some hotels sell discounted park cards to guests—ask.

The **Cinque Terre Trekking Card** costs €7.50 for one day of hiking or €14.50 for two days (covers trails, free use of WCs, park Wi-Fi, and ATC shuttle buses, but not trains).

The **Cinque Terre Treno Card** covers what the Trekking Card does, but also includes local trains connecting all Cinque Terre towns, plus Levanto and La Spezia (€18.20/1 day, €33/2 days, €47/3 days, less off-season, validate card at train station by punching it in the machine, expires at midnight).

Navigation: Park offices hand out a map showing each trail and its number ("SVA" indicates the main coastal trail). Maps aren't essential for the basic coastal path, but for the more challenging routes higher up, you'll want either the park map or one of the commercial maps on sale at park offices for about €5. Trails are usually marked with red and white paint, and often with arrows, trail numbers, and destination names. The word for "path" is *sentiero*.

Hiking Conditions: While the main coastal trail can get strenuous, it's doable for any fit hiker...and the scenery is worth the sweat. But the trails are narrow and rocky, and come with lots of steep, challenging steps. Don't overestimate your abilities. The rocks and

Signs, markers, and arrows help guide hikers on the Cinque Terre's many trails.

metal grates can be slippery in the rain. Flip-flops are not allowed. Pace yourself. For less ambitious walkers, there are great short walks around each town.

Preparation and Safety: Before embarking on the more difficult hikes, get advice from one of the national park offices (located at each train station), or from Cinque Terre Trekking in Manarola (see page 97). The park maintains a map online that shows which trails are open and color-codes them by difficulty—closed (*chiuso*) trails are in black (www.pn5t.it/mappe, then select "Mappa"). Sturdy footwear, a phone for emergencies, plenty of water and snacks, sunscreen (and/or a hat), and a good map are essential.

When to Go: The coastal trail can be extremely crowded and very hot at midday. For the best light, coolest temperatures, and fewer crowds, start your hike early (by 8:00) or late (around 16:00 or 17:00). Before setting out for an evening hike, find out when the sun will set, and leave plenty of time to arrive at your destination before dark; there's no lighting on the trails.

Shuttle Buses: ATC shuttle buses can make the going easier, connecting coastal villages to trailheads higher up. Locals know all the options—and shuttle bus schedules—so ask around. Be aware that shuttles heading into the high country run only in summer, and just once or twice a day. If frustrated with bus schedules, try the local taxis.

Guided Hikes and Excursions: Your park card includes guided hikes and other local excursions (such as town walking tours), which take place almost daily in the summer months. These are announced on the park website (www.parconazionale5terre.it, under "Agenda" or "Initiatives and Events").

Hikes at a Glance

Hikes can be done in either direction. Get local advice before you set out. I've omitted trails closed as of this printing.

Main Coastal Trail

▲▲▲**Vernazza-Monterosso** Challenging but dramatic 2-hour hike, including long stretches of steep steps above Monterosso. See below.

▲▲▲**Corniglia-Vernazza** Most scenic and rewarding segment (1.5 hours) of the main coastal trail, with fine views, significant elevation changes, and moderately challenging stretches on uneven stone steps. See page 25.

Above the Main Coastal Trail

▲▲**Manarola-Corniglia via Volastra** Demanding but gorgeous 2.5-hour hike through vineyards high over the coast; much easier and shorter if you take the shuttle bus from Manarola to Volastra. Park card not required, though it covers the cheap bus ride. See page 26.

▲▲**Madonna di Reggio Sanctuary Hike** Easy 30-minute downhill hike from the sanctuary above Vernazza, best reached by shuttle bus. See page 68.

Top Three Hikes

These three hikes each give the quintessential Cinque Terre hiking experience. The first two are part of the main coastal trail (and require the national park card); the third takes you much higher (and is free).

Main Coastal Trail

▲▲▲Vernazza-Monterosso (2 hours, 2 miles)

The scenic up-and-down-a-lot trek from Vernazza to Monterosso is both challenging and rewarding. The trail is narrow, steep, and crumbly in spots, with a lot of steps, but easy to follow. The views just out of Vernazza, looking back at the town, are spectacular. From there you'll gradually ascend to 550 feet, passing some scenic waterfalls. As you approach Monterosso, you'll descend steeply through vineyards—on very deep, knee-testing stairs—and eventually follow a rivulet to the sea. The last stretch is along a pleasant, paved pathway clinging to the cliff. You'll pop out right at Monterosso's refreshing old-town beach.

High Route Between Porto Venere and Levanto Remote, cliff-capping 22-mile trail (AV5T) high above the main coastal trail and sanctuary trails, best for well-equipped, hardy hikers. See page 30.

Extending the Coastal Trail

To the North

▲**Monterosso-Levanto** A 3.5-hour hike over Punta Mesco; a notch more challenging and longer than other coastal trail segments. See page 31.

▲**Levanto-Bonassola Promenade** Level 30-minute walk that cuts through mountains (largely through tunnels) to connect Levanto to the beach town of Bonassola; fine by foot but better by bike. See page 32.

To the South

▲**Riomaggiore-Porto Venere** Very demanding 6-hour trek high into the hills, ending at picturesque Porto Venere. See page 32.

▲▲▲**Corniglia-Vernazza (1.5 hours, 2 miles)**

The hike from Corniglia to Vernazza—the wildest and greenest section of the coast—is very rewarding but very hilly. From the Corniglia train station, zigzag up to the town (via the steep stairs, the longer road, or the shuttle bus). From Corniglia, you'll reach the trailhead on the main road, past Villa Cecio. You'll hike through vineyards toward Vernazza. After about 10 minutes, you'll see a faded sign for Guvano beach, far beneath you (formerly a nude beach—now closed). The scenic trail continues through lots of fragrant and flowery vegetation into Vernazza. If you need a break before reaching Vernazza, stop at Bar la Torre, with a strip of amazingly scenic and delightfully shady tables perched high above the town.

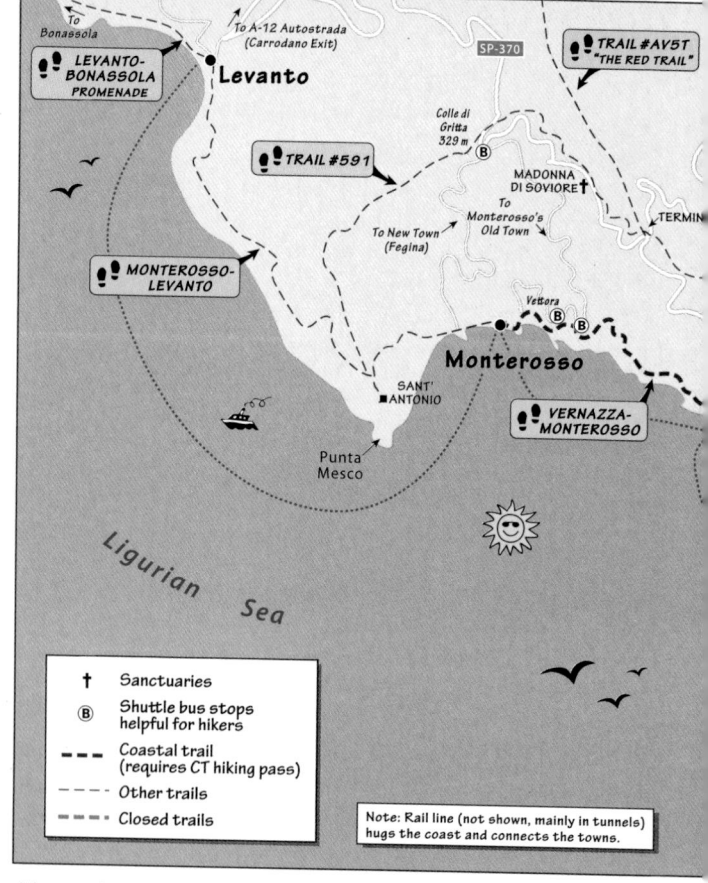

Above the Main Coastal Trail

▲▲**Manarola-Corniglia via Volastra (2.5 hours, 4 miles)**

This challenging hike from Manarola leads up to the village of Volastra, then north through high-altitude vineyard terraces, and steeply down through a forest to Corniglia. You can shave the two

Cinque Terre Hikes

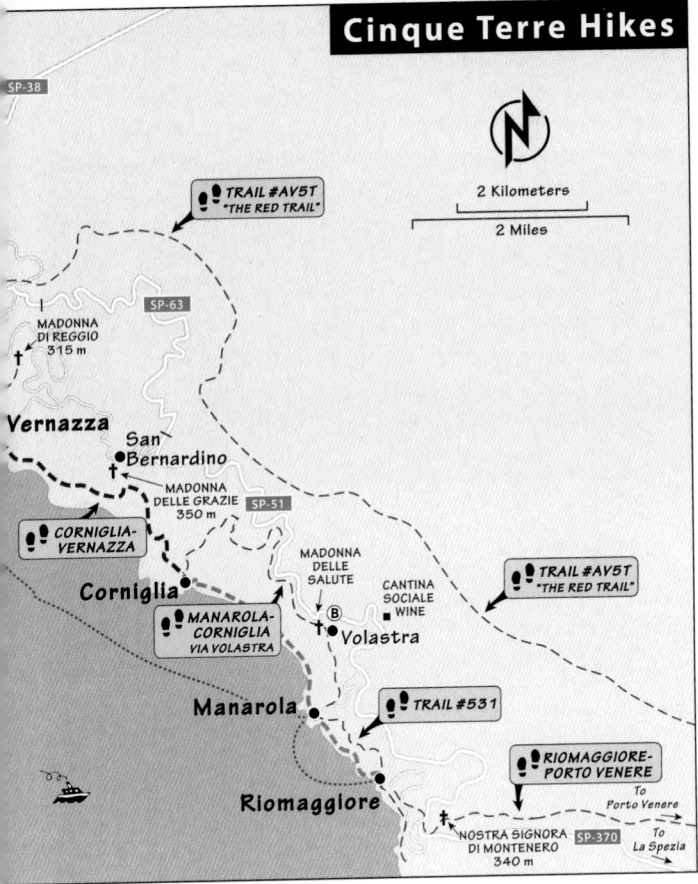

SP-38

TRAIL #AV5T
"THE RED TRAIL"

2 Kilometers

2 Miles

SP-63

MADONNA
DI REGGIO
315 m

Vernazza

San
Bernardino

MADONNA
DELLE GRAZIE SP-51
350 m

CORNIGLIA-
VERNAZZA

MADONNA
DELLE
SALUTE

CANTINA
SOCIALE
• WINE

TRAIL #AV5T
"THE RED TRAIL"

Corniglia

MANAROLA-
CORNIGLIA
VIA VOLASTRA

(B)
Volastra

Manarola

TRAIL #531

RIOMAGGIORE-
PORTO VENERE

Riomaggiore

To
Porto Venere

NOSTRA SIGNORA
DI MONTENERO SP-370
340 m

To
La Spezia

steepest miles off this route by taking the ATC shuttle bus from Manarola up to Volastra (about hourly, 15-minute trip).

If you'd rather hike up to Volastra, you have two options: The more established trail #506 cuts up through the valley; for a more scenic but rougher alternate, take steeper trail #502, which follows the ridge at the top of Manarola's vineyards, with wonderful sea views.

One way to access trail #502 is to begin with the vineyard hike on my self-guided walk for Manarola (page 91); partway along this walk, where you reach the wooden religious scenes scampering up the hillside, take a sharp right and walk uphill, following signs for *Panoramico Volastra (Corniglia)*.

Tiny **Volastra,** perched between Manarola and Corniglia, hosts lots of Germans and Italians in the summer. Its church, Madonna delle Salute, is the sanctuary church for Manarola (as well as the shuttle bus stop). A 20-minute detour from Volastra, in the neighboring hamlet of Groppo, is Cantina Sociale, a cooperative winery open to the public (wine tastings, www.cantinacinqueterre.com).

When you're ready to head on to Corniglia, make your way to the Volastra church and look for *Corniglia* signs. From the front door of the church, directly across the piazza, find the trailhead (marked by an iron cross) for trail #586 to Case Pianca.

Here begins one of the region's finest paths, tightroping along the walled edges of vineyard terraces, with spectacular views over the entire Cinque Terre. You'll cut up and down the terraces a bit—just keep following the red-and-white markings and arrows. After passing a little village (and following signs through someone's seaview

The high trail to Volastra offers breathtaking views.

backyard), the trail enters a forest and begins its sharp, rocky descent into Corniglia. (To skip the descent, backtrack to Volastra and return by shuttle bus to Manarola.) High above Corniglia, you'll reach a fork, where you turn left to proceed downhill on trail #587 to Corniglia.

Other Cinque Terre Walks and Hikes

Beyond the three I've highlighted above, there are dozens of satisfying walks in the Cinque Terre at all levels of difficulty. None of these walks require a park card.

Walks in the Villages

For each Cinque Terre town, I include a **self-guided walk** to help you explore the town (anytime, day or night). My Manarola walk brings you up above town on an easy, rewarding stroll through vineyards with stunning views. In Monterosso, I describe the short huff up to the town's hilltop convent and cemetery. Vernazza's evocative cemetery is also a fairly quick climb from town.

Sanctuary Trails and Other Inland Walks

Each of the five towns has its own chapel or church dedicated to the

You can hike to sanctuaries and cemeteries above each of the five towns.

Virgin Mary, hovering in the hills a mile or two above town and accessible by a long, steep hike (quiet and uncrowded). These sanctuaries were a place of refuge for each village in the age of pirate attacks.

Villagers feel deeply connected to these spiritual retreats, where they remember lost relatives and feel part of a timeless community. In two cases (at Volastra and San Bernardino) the sanctuary church is also the focal point of a small hamlet. In most towns, the shuttle bus can take you from the town center to the sanctuary—you could ride up and hike down (described in each of the next chapters). You can also hike crosswise from one sanctuary to the next (these routes are shown on the park trail map).

Although the flat coastal path between Manarola and Riomaggiore (the Via dell'Amore) remains closed, a steep, challenging route over the bluffs between the two towns, via Beccara, is open (trail #531, taking about an hour).

High Route Between Porto Venere and Levanto

Far above the coastal trails, and higher than the sanctuaries, is the cool, uncrowded 22-mile AV5T trail (*alta via 5 Terre*, also labeled "the red trail"), offering sky-high views over the Cinque Terre seafront. The park rates the trail medium difficulty, but getting up to it (at 2,000 feet) is a demanding climb. This trail continues all the way down to Porto Venere in the south and far beyond the Cinque Terre to the north.

Extending the Coastal Trail

The coastal trail (SVA) continues north of Monterosso and south of Riomaggiore. These stretches are just as scenic and do not require a park card.

To the North

▲ Monterosso-Levanto (3.5 hours, 4 miles)

This strenuous, rugged, and wild hike on the coastal trail (SVA) will take you all the way to Levanto. Wear good shoes and bring lots of water.

Starting from Monterosso, look for signs for the coastal trail at the west end of the new town, and head steeply up. You'll hike up and over Punta Mesco, the bluff that separates the two towns. The first stretch, out of Monterosso, is almost entirely big steps; the rest is mostly a gradual up-and-down.

For a short, scenic detour, look for trail #591 not far out of Monterosso. This brief jog leads to the ruined chapel of Sant'Antonio.

To begin the hike in Levanto, see page 124.

Alternate Route: You can enjoy a higher hike by skipping the steepest stretch and riding one of Monterosso's shuttle buses to Colle di Gritta (and Hotel Monterosso Alto). From there, follow trail #591 along the ridge and down to Colle di Bagari, where several trails intersect. You can follow trail #571c from here or go a little lower to #571—both head down to trail SVA and Levanto. Or, to

A level promenade links Levanto to Bonassola.

make your hike a loop that returns directly to Monterosso, continue from Colle di Bagari along trail #591 to trail SVA, and drop steeply into Monterosso.

▲Levanto-Bonassola (30 minutes)

For an easy excursion, take the train to Levanto, then stroll (or better yet, bike) the level, rails-to-trails promenade to the beach town of Bonassola. With a bike, you can continue farther on, to Framura (see page 124).

To the South

▲Riomaggiore-Porto Venere (6 hours, 8 miles)

For this challenging trek (which has some scary spots if you don't like heights), you'll hike south from Riomaggiore on trail SVA—or on the steep shortcut trail #593—up to the town sanctuary (Nostra Signora di Montenero, or Madonna di Montenero). Then you'll continue up to Colle del Telegrafo, where you join the high AV5T trail that leads all the way down to Porto Venere. Partway along, the town of Campiglia has a little bar/restaurant (and buses to La Spezia).

Monterosso al Mare

Monterosso al Mare is a resort town with a few cars and lots of hotels, rentable beach umbrellas, crowds, and a little more late-night action than the neighboring towns. The only Cinque Terre town with some flat land, Monterosso has two parts: a new town (called Fegina) with a parking lot, train station, and TI; and an old town (*centro storico*), which cradles Old World charm in its small, crooked lanes. In the old town you'll find hole-in-the-wall shops, rustic pastel townscapes, and a new generation of creative small-business owners eager to keep their visitors happy. A handy pedestrian tunnel connects the old with the new.

Strolling the waterfront promenade, you can pick out each of the Cinque Terre towns decorating the coast. After dark, they sparkle. Monterosso is the most enjoyable of the five towns for backpackers or the young-at-heart wanting to connect with others looking for a little nightlife.

Tourist Information

The TI, called Proloco Monterosso, is on the street below the train station (daily 9:00-19:00, mostly closed Nov-March, baggage storage, exit station and go left a few doors to Via Fegina 38, +39 0187 817 506, www.prolocomonterosso.it).

Arrival in Monterosso

By Train: The station is in the new town. Upstairs within the station you'll find a Cinque Terre park office (daily 8:30-19:00, shorter hours off-season) and train ticket windows (daily 6:00-20:00).

The bar along platform 1 (serving salads, sandwiches, and drinks) overlooks both the tracks and the beach, and is a handy place with a cool breeze to hang out while waiting for a train to pull in. As many trains run late, this can turn a frustration into a blessing.

To reach most of my recommended new town hotels, turn right from the station. To get to the old town, turn left from the station, follow the seafront promenade, then duck through the tunnel just before the point—it's a scenic, flat 10-minute stroll.

Taxis usually wait outside the train station, but if not, you can call one (€10 from station to old town, +39 335 616 5842, +39 335 616 5845,

Walk Monterosso's beach promenade…

…or head uphill for an overview.

or +39 335 628 0933). ATC shuttle buses also go to the old town and are cheaper, but only run about once an hour and don't take luggage.

By Car: Monterosso is 30 minutes off the freeway (exit: Carrodano-Levanto). About three miles above Monterosso, there's an intersection where you must choose either *Monterosso Centro Storico* (old part of town) or *Monterosso Fegina* (new town and beachfront parking). Know where you want to go, because you can't drive directly between the new town and old center (the tunnel is closed to most cars). Most drivers should choose the Fegina fork, but get directions from your hotelier.

Parking is easy (except July-Aug and weekends in June) in the new town in the huge beachfront guarded lot (€25/24 hours). In the old town, you'll find the Loreto parking garage on Via Roma, from which it's a 10-minute downhill walk to the main square (€2.50/hour, €25/24 hours).

Helpful Hints

Market: Every Thursday morning (8:00-13:00), trucks pull in to the old town and fill the public area by the beach with stalls selling produce and more.

Baggage Storage: The **TI** will store bags (€5-8/day).

Pharmacy: You'll find one at Via Fegina 42, next to the train station (Mon-Fri, closed Sat-Sun, +39 0187 818 391).

Laundry: For full-service, same-day laundry in the new town, try **Wash and Dry Lavarapido.** They'll pick up at your hotel, or you can drop it at their shop. The owners speak little English, so ask your hotelier to arrange the details (daily 8:00-19:00, Via Molinelli 17, +39 339 484 0940, Lucia and Ivano). In the old town, head uphill to **Luètu Lavanderia,** by the post office (daily 8:00-18:00, Via Roma 86, +39 0187 765 354).

Massage: Physiotherapist **Giorgio Moggia** gives good massages (€70/hour, +39 339 314 6127, giomogg@tin.it).

MONTEROSSO WALKS

These self-guided walks will introduce you to Monterosso. The first one, focusing on the mostly level town center, takes about 30 minutes. For the second one, you'll summit the adjacent hill—allow an hour or so.

Monterosso Harbor and Town Walk

▶ Hike out from the dock in the old town and stand atop the concrete breakwater. (If you're arriving by boat, you'll disembark here.)

Breakwater

From this point you can survey Monterosso's old town (straight ahead) and new town (stretching to the left, with train station and parking lot). Notice the bluff that separates old and new, and imagine how much harder your commute would be if the narrow road tethering these two towns were somehow cut off. It happened in the spring of 2013, when the wall below the hill-topping Capuchin church gave way in a landslide. For a time, the only way to connect the two halves of town by car was to drive six miles around; on foot, you had to hike up and over this hill.

Looking to the right, you can see all *cinque* of the *terre* from one spot: Vernazza, Corniglia (above the shore), Manarola, and a few buildings of Riomaggiore beyond that.

These days, the harbor hosts more paddleboats than fishing boats. Erosion is a major problem. The partial breakwater—the row of giant rocks in the middle of the harbor—is designed to save the beach from washing away. While old-timers remember a vast beach, their grandchildren truck in sand each spring to give tourists something to bask on. (The Nazis liked the Cinque Terre, too—find two of their bomb-hardened bunkers embedded in the bluff.)

The fancy four-star Hotel Porto Roca (the pink building high on the hill, on the far right of the harbor) marks the trail to Vernazza. High above, you see an example of the costly roads built in the 1980s to connect the Cinque Terre towns with the freeway over the hills.

The two prominent capes (Punta di Montenero to the right, and Punta Mesco to the left) define the Cinque Terre region. The closer Punta Mesco is part of a protected marine sanctuary and home to a rare sea grass that provides an ideal home for fish eggs. Buoys keep

Arriving in Monterosso by boat

Church of St. John the Baptist

fishing boats away. The cape was once a quarry, providing employ-ment to locals who chipped out the stones used to build the local towns (the greenish stones making up part of the breakwater are from there).

On the far end of the new town, marking the best free beach around, you can just see the statue named *Il Gigante* (hard to spot be-cause it blends in with the gray rock). It's 45 feet tall and once held a trident. While it looks as if it were hewn from the rocky cliff, it's actually made of reinforced concrete and dates from the beginning of the 20th century, when it supported a dance terrace for a *fin de siècle* villa. A violent storm left the giant holding nothing but memories of Monterosso's glamorous age.

▶ *From the breakwater, walk toward the old town and under the train tracks. Then venture right into the square and find the statue of a dan-dy holding what looks like a box cutter (behind the big playground).*

Piazza Garibaldi

The statue honors Giuseppe Garibaldi, the dashing firebrand revolu-tionary who, in the 1860s, helped unite the people of Italy into a mod-ern nation. Facing Garibaldi, with your back to the sea, you'll see (on your right) the orange City Hall (with the European Union flag beside the Italian one).

Just under the bell tower (with your back to the sea, it's on your left), a set of covered arcades facing the sea is where the old-timers hang out (they see all and know all). The crenellated bell tower marks the church; it was originally the tower of a fortified gate.

▶ *Go to church.*

Monterosso al Mare

Accommodations

1. Hotel Villa Steno
2. Il Giardino Incantato
3. Hotel Pasquale
4. Buranco Agriturismo
5. Locanda il Maestrale
6. Hotel la Colonnina
7. Albergo Marina
8. Manuel's Guesthouse
9. L'Antica Terrazza & Gastronomia"San Martino"
10. Albergo al Carugio
11. La Villa degli Argentieri
12. To Hotel Villa Adriana
13. Hotel la Spiaggia & Bar Giò
14. A Cà du Gigante
15. Hotel Punta Mesco
16. Raffaella Viviani Rooms

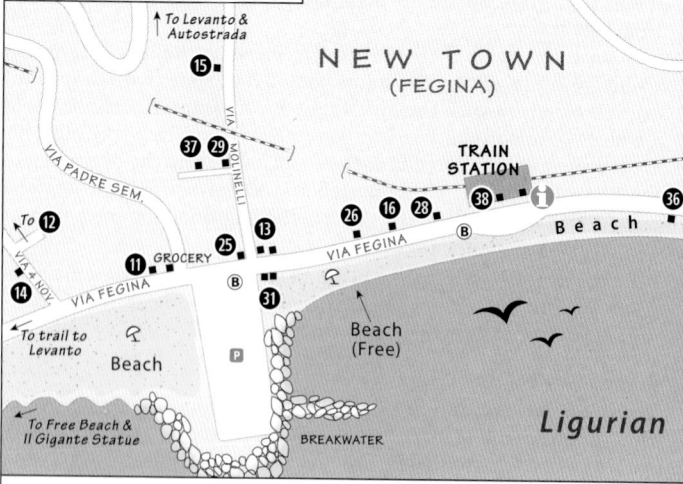

Eateries & Nightlife

17. Ristorante Belvedere
18. Il Casello
19. L'Ancora della Tortuga & Torre Aurora
20. Via Venti & Bakery
21. L'Osteria & Emy's Way
22. Ristorante al Pozzo
23. Ciak
24. La Smorfia & Pasticceria Laura
25. Miky
26. La Cantina di Miky
27. Il Frantoio Focacceria
28. Il Massimo della Focaccia

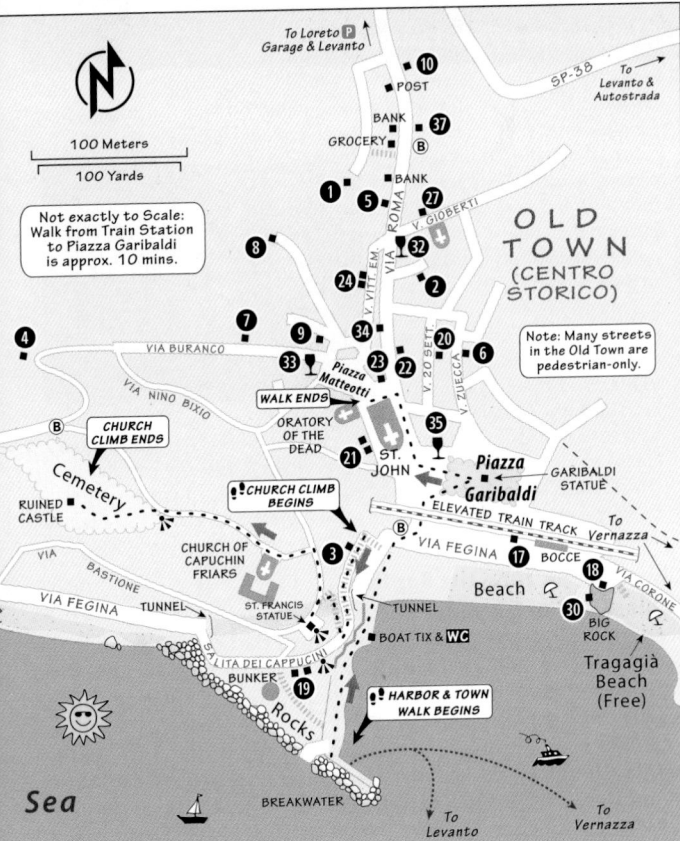

To Loreto P
Garage & Levanto

SP-38
To
Levanto &
Autostrada

10
POST

BANK
37
GROCERY
B
BANK

N

100 Meters
100 Yards

Not exactly to Scale:
Walk from Train Station
to Piazza Garibaldi
is approx. 10 mins.

1
5
27

OLD
TOWN
(CENTRO
STORICO)

V. GIOBERTI

V. ROMA

8

32

V. VITT. EM.

24
2

Note: Many streets
in the Old Town are
pedestrian-only.

7

4

9
34
20
6

VIA BURANCO
33
23
22

V. ZUECCA
V. 20 SETT.

VIA NINO BIXIO
Piazza
Matteotti

WALK ENDS

B
CHURCH CLIMB ENDS

35

Cemetery

ORATORY
OF THE
DEAD

RUINED
CASTLE

CHURCH CLIMB
BEGINS

21
ST.
JOHN

Piazza
Garibaldi

GARIBALDI
STATUE

VIA
BASTIONE

CHURCH OF
CAPUCHIN
FRIARS

3

ELEVATED TRAIN TRACK
To
Vernazza

B
VIA FEGINA

17
BOCCE

VIA CORONE

VIA FEGINA
TUNNEL

ST. FRANCIS
STATUE

TUNNEL

Beach
18

30
BIG
ROCK

BOAT TIX & WC

SALITA DEI CAPPUCINI

Tragagià
Beach
(Free)

BUNKER
19

Rocks

HARBOR & TOWN
WALK BEGINS

Sea

BREAKWATER

To
Levanto

To
Vernazza

29 La Bottega
30 Beach Bar Alga
31 Bar il Baretto & Stella
Marina Beach Bar
32 Enoteca Internazionale
Wine Tasting
33 Enoteca da Eliseo

34 Fast Bar
35 El Dorado Wine Bar
36 La Terrazza Cigolini
37 Launderette (2)
38 Pharmacy

Cinque Terre Flood and Recovery

On October 25, 2011, after a dry summer, a heavy rainstorm hit the Cinque Terre. Within four hours, 22 inches of rain fell. Flash floods rushed down the hillsides, picking up mud, rocks, trees, furniture, and even cars and buses in their raging, destructive path through the streets down to the sea. Part of Monterosso's old town and Vernazza's main drag were buried under a dozen feet of mud. Four villagers from Vernazza lost their lives.

Today, the Cinque Terre is back to normal. Most visitors wouldn't even notice that in the affected areas of Monterosso and Vernazza, everything is new: stoves, tables, chairs, and plates. Strolling through these towns today, appreciate the resilience of the human spirit (and the importance of good drainage).

Church of St. John the Baptist (Chiesa di San Giovanni Battista)

First, walk along the side the church. Near the second side door, find the high-water mark (*altezza massima*) from an October 1966 flood, which also famously devastated Florence. Nearby, a second (higher) plaque commemorates the 2011 flood.

Now hook left, around the church, and appreciate its striped main facade. Alternating white marble from Carrara and green marble from Punta Mesco, the stripes get narrower the higher they go, creating the illusion that the church is taller than it really is. The church is typical of the region's Gothic style. Note the lacy, stone rose window above the entrance—considered one of the finest in northern Italy. It's as delicate as crochet work, with 18 slender columns (creating the petals of the rose).

Step inside for more Ligurian Gothic: original marble columns and capitals with pointed arches to match. The octagonal baptismal font (in the back of the church) was carved from Carrara marble in 1359. Imagine the job getting that from the quarries, about 40 miles away. The fine Baroque altar was crafted with various marbles from around Italy in the 1700s. The church itself dates from 1307—the proud inscription on the left-middle column reads "MilloCCCVII."

▶ *Leaving the church, turn left and go to church again.*

Oratory of the Dead (Oratorio dei Neri)

During the Counter-Reformation, the Catholic Church offset the rising influence of Protestantism by creating brotherhoods of good works. These religious Rotary clubs were called "confraternities." Monterosso had two, nicknamed White and Black. This building is the oratory of the Black group, whose mission—as the macabre decor filling the interior indicates—was to arrange for funerals and take care of widows, orphans, the shipwrecked, and the souls of those who ignore the request for a €1 donation. It dates from the 16th century, and membership has passed from father to son for generations. Notice the fine, carved pews (c. 1700) and the haunted-house chandeliers. Look up at the ceiling to find the symbol of the confraternity: a skull-and-crossbones and an hourglass...death awaits us all.

▶ *On that cheery note, if you're in a lazy mood, you can end your walking tour here to enjoy strolling, shopping, gelato-licking, a day at the beach... or all of the above. But if you're up for a hike, face out to sea, look to the right, and imagine the view from the top of that hill. Now...go see it.*

Capuchin Church and Climb

The hill that separates the old town from the new rewards anyone who climbs up with a peaceful church, a cemetery in the clouds, and a panoramic view.

▶ *From the old town's beachfront, find the brick steps squeezed between Hotel Pasquale and its restaurant, and start climbing. The lane is signed* Salita dei Cappuccini, *but in the local dialect it's called* Zii di Frati, *or...*

Switchbacks of the Friars

Follow the yellow brick road (OK, it's not yellow...but I couldn't help singing as I skipped skyward). Several switchbacks up, above the seaside castle, detour left to the statue of St. Francis and a wolf taking in a grand view. Enjoy an opportunity to see all five of the Cinque Terre towns. Then backtrack 20 yards to the switchback and continue uphill.

▶ *When you reach a gate marked* Convento e Chiesa Cappuccini, *you have arrived at the...*

St. Francis graces a Ligurian Sea viewpoint.

Church of the Capuchin Friars

Walk through the gate and up the stairs into the church courtyard. The former monastery is now manned by a single caretaker friar. (If you meet Father Renato, take a moment to speak with him—he's a joyful soul who loves to connect.) Before stepping inside, notice the church's striped Romanesque facade. It's all fake. Tap it—no marble, just cheap 18th-century stucco. Go inside and sit in the rear pew. The high altarpiece painting of St. Francis can be rolled up on special days to reveal a statue of Mary standing behind it.

The fine painting of the **Crucifixion (on the left)** recalls how, when Jesus died, the earth went dark. Notice the eclipsed sun in the painting, just to the right of the cross.

▶ *Leave and turn left through another gate to hike 100 yards uphill to the cemetery filling the ruined castle at the top of the hill. Reaching the cemetery's gate, look back and enjoy the view over the town.*

Cemetery in the Ruined Castle

In the Dark Ages, the village huddled behind this castle. As the threat of pirates passed, it slowly expanded to the waterfront. Notice the town view from here—no sea. You're looking at the oldest part of Monterosso, tucked behind the hill, out of view of 13th-century pirates.

Respectfully explore the cemetery. Ponder the black-and-white photos of grandparents past. Read the headstones: *Q.R.P.* is *Qui Riposa in Pace* (i.e., *R.I.P.*). Rich families had their own little tomb buildings. The fresh flowers show how much people treasure this place.

Climb to the very summit—the castle's keep, or place of last refuge. Priests are buried in a line of graves closest to the sea, but facing inland, looking toward the town's holy sanctuary high on the hillside (above the road, with its triangular steeple just peeking above the trees). Each Cinque Terre town has a lofty sanctuary, dedicated to Mary and dear to the village hearts.

▶ *Your tour is over—any trail leads you back into town.*

EXPERIENCES IN MONTEROSSO

Hikes from Monterosso

For a relatively easy in-town hike, take a rewarding climb up to the **hill-top cemetery** between the old and the new towns (described earlier).

The most popular hike from Monterosso is to **Vernazza** on the main coastal trail; you'll need a park card (sold at the trailhead or at park offices). The hike to **Levanto** is free, either over the Punta Mesco bluff on the main SVA trail, or on another route where you first take the bus up to Colle di Gritta—which makes most of the rest of the hike downhill.

Another option is path #509 between Monterosso and its **Madonna di Soviore sanctuary** (you could take the shuttle bus up and walk down). From Soviore you could hike to Vernazza's **Madonna di Reggio sanctuary,** following a mostly level trail (#591) to Termine, then down to Madonna di Reggio (on #582), and then, if you wish, steeply downhill into Vernazza (on #508). Allow 2.5 hours to Vernazza on this route if you start with the shuttle bus to Soviore. (For more on these hikes, see page 24.)

Beaches

Monterosso's **new town** has easily the Cinque Terre's best—and most crowded—beach (immediately in front of the train station). Most of the beach is technically private, where (at Stella Marina) you'll pay €35 to rent two chairs and an umbrella for the day (prices get soft in the

Monterosso's sandy new town beach is busy.

The gravel old town beach is less crowded.

afternoon). Light lunches are served by beach cafés to sunbathers at their lounge chairs. Various outfits along here rent kayaks and stand-up paddleboards (look for signs at the west end of the beach—near the parking lot—or ask around). If there are no umbrellas on a stretch of beach, it's public (free), so you can spread out a towel anywhere. There's a free beach at the far west end, near the Gigante statue; others are marked on the "Monterosso al Mare" map, earlier.

The **old town** also has its own predominantly private beach; rent umbrellas, chairs, kayaks, and paddleboats from Beach Bar Alga, which is also a scenic spot for a drink. Tucked just beyond the private beach—under the Il Casello restaurant at the east end of town—is the free public beach called *Tragagià*, which is gravelly and generally less crowded (showers). The bocce ball court (next to Il Casello) is busy with older men enjoying their favorite pastime.

Wine Tasting

Buranco Agriturismo is one of the largest producers of wines in the Cinque Terre, with tastings on their terrace overlooking the vineyards. You'll try some of their wines, plus grappa (firewater), *limoncino,* and some light snacks (about €40/person). Another option is "wine trekking," where you get a picnic basket and audioguide and set off on a walk around the grounds (€50/couple, call or email to arrange). You can also taste their wines over lunch or dinner—see "Eating in Monterosso," later (follow Via Buranco uphill to path, 10 minutes above town, also rents rooms, +39 349 434 8046, www.burancocinqueterre.it, info@buranco.it, Mary).

Enoteca Internazionale is a good place in town to sample local wines. Mario, Susanna, and Valentina serve a selection of five wines for €20 (his bruschetta makes a fine light meal as you're sipping, open daily until late, Via Roma 62, +39 0187 817 278, www.enotecainternazionale.com).

Boat Rides

In addition to the regularly scheduled big boats (see page 18), you can hire your own captain for transfers to other towns or for a lazy sightseeing cruise (if the water's calm).

Stefano has a six-person boat, the *Matilde* (about €100/hour, 2 hours is enough for a quick spin and swimming; 5-hour trips to Porto Venere and offshore islands possible; +39 333 821 2007, www.matildenavigazione.com, info@matildenavigazione.com).

Fish & Chill offers five-hour daytime excursions on a cushy boat that carries nine (departs about 10:30, €150/person). Expect snorkeling, village visits, and a buffet lunch. They also do sunset tours and private groups (+39 340 834 7834, www.cinqueterreboat.com, 5terretourfishandchill@gmail.com, Diego and Silvia).

Sea Breeze Boat Tours arranges day and *aperitivo* sunset tours and will shuttle you to any of the coastal towns. They also run tours from Levanto (€85-140/person, +39 328 824 6889 or +39 338 809 9278, www.seabreezeboattours.com, info@seabreezeboattours.com, Matteo and Federica).

NIGHTLIFE IN MONTEROSSO

Although I've listed these establishments for their nightlife, they work any time of day for a drink and spot to relax.

Enoteca da Eliseo, my favorite wine bar in town, comes with operatic ambience. Eliseo and his wife, Mary, love music and wine. Taste by the glass (*bicchiere*), or select a fine bottle from their shop shelf, then enjoy the wine, a few included nibbles, and views of the village action from their cozy tables. Eliseo stocks more than a hundred varieties of grappa (Wed-Mon 10:00-23:00, closed Tue, Piazza Matteotti 3, a block inland behind church, +39 0187 817 308).

Fast Bar is super basic, but it's the best bar in town for young travelers and night owls. Customers mix travel tales with big, cold beers, and the crowd (and the rock 'n' roll) gets noisier as the night rolls on. Come here to watch sports on TV all day (cheap *panini*, pizza, salads, and other light meals usually served until midnight, open 7:00-late, in the old town at Via Roma 13, +39 0187 819 278; Alex, Francesco, and Stefano).

La Cantina di Miky, in the new town just beyond the train station, is a trendy bar-restaurant with an extensive cocktail and grappa menu. The seating is in three zones: overlooking the beach, in the garden, or in the cellar. Try the fun "five villages" wine tasting. This is the best place in town for top-end Italian microbrews (Thu-Tue until late, closed Wed, Via Fegina 90, +39 0187 802 525). It's also recommended for dining (see listing under "Eating in Monterosso," later).

El Dorado Wine Bar is the local old-town nighttime hangout. Set on a small piazza, it offers music, drinks, pizza, and people-watching late into the night (Piazza Garibaldi 22, daily 10:00-2:00 in the morning, +39 331 475 9611).

Beach Bars: On a balmy evening, enjoy a memorable drink with a view of swimmers, sunbathers, and the languid Ligurian Sea. In the new town, try **La Terrazza Cigolini,** overlooking the beach by the big rock. In the old town, **Beach Bar Alga** has an island ambience (all outside, daily until 20:00, Stefano).

Monterosso's beachfront is beautiful on a balmy evening.

SLEEPING IN MONTEROSSO

Monterosso, the most beach-resorty of the five Cinque Terre towns, offers maximum comfort and ease. Rooms in Monterosso are a better value than similar rooms in crowded Vernazza, and the proprietors tend to be more genuine and welcoming.

In the Old Town

$$$$ **Hotel Villa Steno** is lovingly managed and features great view balconies, panoramic gardens, a roof terrace with sun beds, and the friendly help of Matteo and his wife, Carla. Of their 16 rooms, 14 have view balconies (RS%, air-con, family rooms, hearty buffet breakfast, elevator, laundry service, ask about pay parking when you reserve, hike up to their panoramic terrace, cooking classes, Via Roma 109, +39 0187 817 028 or +39 0187 818 336, www.villasteno.com, steno@pasini. com). It's a 15-minute climb (or €10 taxi ride) from the train station to the hotel. My readers get a free Cinque Terre info packet and a glass of local wine when they check in—ask.

$$$$ **Il Giardino Incantato** ("The Enchanted Garden") is a charming, comfortable four-room B&B in a tastefully renovated 16th-century Ligurian home in the heart of the old town. It's run by kind and eager-to-please Fausto and Mariapia and their gregarious staff. Sip their homemade *limoncino* at *aperitivo* time, and have breakfast under lemon trees in the delightful hidden garden that's candlelit in the evening (air-con, free minibar and tea-and-coffee service, laundry, Via Mazzini 18, +39 0187 818 315, mobile +39 333 264 9252, www. ilgiardinoincantato.net, giardino_incantato@libero.it).

$$$$ **Hotel Pasquale** is modern and comfortable with 15 seaview rooms (nine with balconies), run by the same family as Hotel Villa Steno (listed above). Located right on the harbor, it's just a few steps from the beach, boat dock, and tunnel to the new town. While there is some train noise, the soundtrack is mostly a lullaby of waves. Marco's photographs decorate the breakfast room (RS%, family room, air-con, elevator, laundry service, cooking demonstrations, closed Nov-Feb, Via Fegina 4, +39 0187 817 550 or +39 0187 817 477, www.hotelpasquale. it, pasquale@pasini.com, welcoming Felicita and Marco). Felicita also rents several well-equipped apartments in the center of the old town.

$$$$ **Buranco Agriturismo,** a 10-minute hike above the old

town, has wonderful gardens and views over a hidden valley draped with vineyards and lemon groves. Along with their recommended restaurant and wine and olive-oil production, they offer three rooms and three apartments, with breakfast served on a covered terrace. It's a rare opportunity to stay in a farmhouse yet be able to walk to town (air-con, free parking, +39 349 434 8046, www.burancocinqueterre.it, info@buranco.it, informally run by Loredana, Mary, and Irene).

$$$ Locanda il Maestrale rents six stylish rooms in a sophisticated and peaceful little inn. Although renovated with all the modern comforts and thoughtful details, it retains centuries-old character under frescoed ceilings. Its peaceful sun terrace overlooking the old town and Via Roma action is a delight. Guests enjoy complimentary drinks and snacks each afternoon (air-con, Via Roma 37, +39 0187 817 013, mobile +39 338 4530 531, www.locandamaestrale.net, maestrale@monterossonet.com, Stefania and Giovanni).

$$$ Hotel la Colonnina has 22 big rooms, all but one with a private terrace. The generous and meticulously cared-for public spaces include a cozy garden and an inviting shared seaview terrace with sun beds. It's buried in the town's fragrant and sleepy back streets (family rooms, air-con, fridges, elevator, a block inland from main square at Via Zuecca 6, +39 0187 817 439, www.lacolonninacinqueterre.it, info@lacolonninacinqueterre.it, Cristina).

$$$ Albergo Marina, run by enthusiastic husband-and-wife team Marina and Eraldo, has 23 pleasant rooms and a garden with lemon trees. They serve a good breakfast, provide lots of little extras, and offer a fine value (RS%, family rooms, elevator, air-con, fridges, kayak and snorkel equipment, Via Buranco 40, +39 0187 817 613, www.hotelmarina5terre.com, marina@hotelmarina5terre.com).

$$$ Manuel's Guesthouse, perched high above the town among terraces, is a garden getaway run by Lorenzo and his father, Giovanni. They have six big, artfully decorated rooms and a grand view. After climbing the killer stairs from the town center, their killer terrace is hard to leave—especially after a few drinks (cash only, air-con, up about 100 steps behind church—you can ask Lorenzo to carry your bags up the hill, Via San Martino 39, +39 333 439 0809, www.manuelsguesthouse.com, manuelsguesthouse@libero.it).

$$ L'Antica Terrazza rents four tight, classy rooms right in town. With a pretty terrace overlooking the pedestrian street,

Raffaella and Jon offer a good deal (RS%, one single has private bath down the hall, air-con, Vicolo San Martino 1, +39 347 132 6213, www.anticaterrazza.com, post@anticaterrazza.com).

$$ Albergo al Carugio has nine practical rooms in a big apartment-style building with a small patio at the top of the old town. It's quiet, comfy, and a fine budget value; one room has a private terrace (RS%, no breakfast, air-con, fridges, Via Roma 100, +39 0187 817 453, mobile +39 328 847 6276, www.alcarugio.it, info@alcarugio.it, conscientiously run by kindly Andrea).

In the New Town

$$$$ La Villa degli Argentieri offers 11 spacious rooms, six with balconies, from a choice position at the quiet end of the new town's beachfront street. From the front rooms you'll get a peek-a-boo look (through trees) at the water, but the inviting rooftop breakfast terrace has panoramic views (air-con, elevator, Via Fegina 120, +39 0187 916 295, www.villaargentieri.it, info@villaargentieri.it).

$$$$ Hotel Villa Adriana is big, contemporary, and bright, set on a church-owned estate with a peaceful garden, a pool, free parking (reserve ahead), and a no-stress style. They rent 55 sterile rooms—most with terraces, a few with sea views (family rooms, air-con, elevator, free loaner bikes, affordable dinners, Via IV Novembre 23, +39 0187 818 109, www.villaadriana.info, info@villaadriana.info).

$$$$ Hotel la Spiaggia, facing the beach, is a venerable place with 19 rooms (half with sea views) and a quiet garden retreat (air-con, elevator, free parking—reserve in advance, Via Lungomare 96, +39 0187 817 567, www.laspiaggiahotel.it, laspiaggiahotel@gmail.com, run by Maria). They also rent four pricey, ultra-mod rooms in a small building on the seafront promenade.

$$$$ A Cà du Gigante, despite its name, is a tiny yet chic refuge with nine rooms, most on the ground floor. About 100 yards from the beach (and surrounded by blocky apartments), the interior is tastefully done with upscale comfort in mind (air-con, limited pay parking—reserve ahead, Via IV Novembre 11, +39 0187 817 401, www.ilgigantecinqueterre.it, gigante@ilgigantecinqueterre.it, Claudia).

$$$ Hotel Punta Mesco is a tidy, well-run little haven renting 17 quiet, casual rooms at a good price. While none have views, 10 rooms have small terraces (family room, air-con, parking, Via Molinelli 35,

+39 0187 817 495, www.hotelpuntamesco.it, info@hotelpuntamesco.it, Roberto, Diego, and Manuel).

$$ Raffaella Viviani rents five basic, dated, but affordable rooms up a single flight of stairs from the beachfront road. Three rooms face the sea (two with small balconies); two have terraces overlooking a garden (big family rooms, cash only, no breakfast, air-con, Via Fegina 84, +39 329 336 9577, www.affittacamerevivianiraffaella.it, lella-v71@ hotmail.it).

EATING IN MONTEROSSO

With a Sea View

$$ Ristorante Belvedere, big and sprawling, serves good-value meals indoors or outdoors on the harborfront. Their huge €52 *anfora belvedere*—mixed seafood stew dumped dramatically at the table from a pottery amphora into your bowl—can easily be split among up to four diners. Another fishy treat, their €20 *misto mare* plate, nearly makes an entire meal for two. Mussel fans will enjoy the *tagliolini della casa*. It's energetically run by Federico and Roberto (Wed-Mon 12:00-14:30 & 18:00-22:00, closed Tue, on the harbor in the old town, +39 0187 817 033).

$$ Il Casello offers outdoor terrace seating only, on a little bluff overlooking the old town beach when the weather's nice. It's a pleasant spot for pasta, seafood, or a drink (daily 12:00-22:00, +39 333 492 7629, Bacco and Gianfranco).

$$$ L'Ancora della Tortuga is a top option in Monterosso for sea-view elegance, with gorgeous outdoor seating high on a bluff and a white-tablecloth-and-candles interior fit for an admiral. Drop by to choose and reserve a table for later. Consider their €40 tasting *menu* (Tue-Sun 12:30-15:30 & 18:30-21:30, closed Mon and when stormy; at the tip of the point between the old and new towns—just outside the tunnel; +39 0187 800 065, mobile +39 333 240 7956, Silvia and Giamba).

$$$$ Torre Aurora is a top-end, fancy restaurant with no indoor seating. You'll dine outside (wrapped in a blanket if it's cold) around the medieval tower with commanding views of the sea while enjoying simple yet creative dishes. Reservations are smart (daily from 12:30 in good weather, +39 366 145 3702, www.torreauroracinqueterre.com, Elia). They serve cocktails outside of mealtime.

In the Old Town

$$$$ Via Venti is a quiet little trattoria, hidden on a traffic-free street deep in the heart of the old town, where chef Ilaria and her husband, Michele, create and serve imaginative seafood dishes. Eat indoors or out; you'll be tempted by their delicate and savory gnocchi with crab, tender ravioli stuffed with fresh fish, and pear-and-pecorino pasta (Fri-Wed 12:00-14:30 & 18:30-22:30, closed Thu, Via XX Settembre 32, +39 0187 818 347).

$$$ Buranco Agriturismo, just 10 minutes' walk uphill from the old town, feels like another world. You'll eat on a heated covered terrace, overlooking their beautiful grounds and forested hillsides. Chef Giovanni is proud of his shrimp risotto, spaghetti with anchovies, and sophisticated fish and meat courses; they serve their own wines (air-con, free parking, reservations wise, also has rooms, +39 349 434 8046, www.burancocinqueterre.it, Mary).

$ Gastronomia "San Martino," warmly run by hard-working Moreno and Sabrina, is a tiny, humble combination of takeaway and sit-down café with surprisingly affordable, quality dishes. Belly up to the glass case and see what's cooking, then eat at one of the few tables—inside or out on a pleasant street. You're welcome to create your own €15 mixed plate by pointing to whatever appeals (Tue-Sun 12:00-15:00 & 18:00-21:30, closed Mon, next to recommended L'Antica Terrazza hotel at Vicolo San Martino 3, +39 346 109 7338).

$$ L'Osteria is a delightful little family-run place serving "cuisine with passion" at wonderful prices. Alessandro thoughtfully explains your options and Elisa is understandably proud of her cakes. Their Possa wine, from vineyards close to the sea, is the oyster of local wines, or maybe it's just the Ligurian music (Tue-Sun lunch served 12:00-14:30, evening seatings at 19:00 and 21:00, closed Mon, Via Vittorio Emanuele 5, +39 0187 819 224). It's a cozy scene inside with a few tables outside in the shadow of the church.

$$$ Ristorante al Pozzo is a favorite among locals. It's family-run, with good old-fashioned quality, as Gino (with his long white beard) cooks, and his English-speaking son, Manuel, serves. They have one of the best wine lists in town, serve only homemade pasta, and are known for their raw fish and wonderful seafood *antipasti misti* (Fri-Wed 12:00-15:00 & 18:30-22:30, closed Thu, Via Roma 24, +39 0187 817 575).

$$$ Ciak, high-energy and tightly packed—inside and out—is a local institution with reliably good food and (sometimes) a bit of an attitude. Stroll a couple of paces past the outdoor tables up Via Roma to see what Signore Ciak (who wears his Popeye cap in the kitchen) has on the stove (Thu-Tue 12:00-15:00 & 18:00-22:30, closed Wed, Piazza Don Minzoni 6, +39 0187 817 014, www.ristoranteciak.net).

$ La Smorfia—a local favorite—cooks up good pizza in a sloppy setting that somehow says, "Great pizza enjoyed here." Their large pizzas can feed three (Wed-Mon 11:00-24:00, closed Tue, Via Vittorio Emanuele 73, +39 0187 818 395).

In the New Town

$$$$ Miky is packed with a well-dressed clientele who know their seafood. For elegantly presented, top-quality food that celebrates local ingredients and traditions, it's worth the steep prices. It's a proud family operation—Miky (dad), Simonetta (mom), charming Sara (daughter, who greets guests)—and the attentive waitstaff all work hard. Many of their fine wines are available by the glass. Their mixed dessert sampler plate, *dolce misto,* serves two and is a fitting capper (Wed-Mon 12:00-15:00 & 19:00-23:00, closed Tue, reservations wise, in the new town 100 yards from train station at Via Fegina 104, +39 0187 817 608, www.ristorantemiky.it).

$$$ La Cantina di Miky, a few doors down from the station, serves artfully crafted Ligurian specialties that follow in Miky's family tradition of quality. Run by son Manuel—and Christine from New Jersey—it's youthful and informal (but reservations are still wise—sit downstairs, in the garden, or on the promenade overlooking the sea). The €23 anchovy tasting plate is an education (creative desserts, large selection of Italian microbrews, Thu-Tue 12:00-15:00 & 19:00-22:00, closed Wed, Via Fegina 90, +39 0187 802 525). This place doubles as a cocktail bar in the evenings.

Light Meals, Takeout Food, and Breakfast

In the Old Town: Lots of shops sell pizza and focaccia to eat in or take out for an easy picnic on the beach or trail. At **$ Il Frantoio Focacceria,** Simone makes tasty pizza and focaccia (Fri-Wed 9:00-14:00 & 16:30-20:00, closed Thu, just off Via Roma at Via Gioberti 1). **$ Emy's Way** offers pasta, thick-crust pizza, and deep-fried seafood in to-go cones (daily 12:00-22:00, along the skinny street next to the church, +39 331 788 1088, Emiliano).

In the New Town: For a quick bite right under the train station (or to take over to the beach), try **$ Il Massimo della Focaccia** for its quiche-like tortes, sandwiches, focaccia pizzas, and desserts. There are benches just in front—a good bet for a light meal with a sea view (Thu-Tue 9:00-19:00, closed Wed, Via Fegina 50). **La Bottega** is Monterosso's largest grocery store, a smart minimart with fresh produce, *antipasti,* deli items, and other picnic fare. They'll make you a sandwich: Select a bread and filling, and pay by weight (Mon-Sat 8:00-13:00 & 16:30-19:00, closed Sun, Via Molinelli 9).

Breakfast: Most hotels include breakfast in the room rate, but a handful leave you to your own devices. In the **old town,** for breakfast on the beach, try **Beach Bar Alga** (from 8:00 when the weather's nice). For the freshest bakery items, follow your nose to **Pasticceria Laura,** serving coffee and pastries daily from 7:00 (Via Vittorio Emanuele 59). There's a **bakery** at Via XX Settembre 26, next to the recommended Via Venti restaurant.

In the **new town,** these places (on Via Fegina, near Hotel la Spiaggia) serve something akin to breakfast starting at 8:00: **Bar Giò** (bacon and eggs), **Bar il Baretto** (bacon and eggs), and **Stella Marina Beach Bar** (croissants and yogurt—served down on the beach). Your best bet might be a picnic breakfast from the tiny *alimentari*/supermarket at Via Fegina 116 (cheeses, breads, pastries, and fruit).

MONTEROSSO CONNECTIONS

Of the five Cinque Terre towns, Monterosso has the most direct train connections with towns outside the Cinque Terre.

From Monterosso by Train to: Levanto (3-4/hour, 5 minutes), **Sestri Levante** (at least hourly, 30-40 minutes, most trains to Genoa stop here), **Santa Margherita Ligure** (at least hourly, 50-60 minutes, often with a change in Sestri Levante), **Genoa** (at least hourly, 1.5 hours, often with 1 change; change trains here for destinations in France), **Milan** (5-6/day direct, 3 hours, more with changes), **Venice** (at least hourly, 6 hours, 1-3 changes, simplest to change in Milan), **La Spezia** (2-3/hour, 15-30 minutes), **Pisa** (at least hourly, 1-1.5 hours, most change in La Spezia), **Rome** (every 1-2 hours, 4.5 hours, change in La Spezia).

Vernazza

With the closest thing to a natural harbor—overseen by a ruined castle, a stout stone church, and a pastel canyon of fisherfolk homes—Vernazza is the jewel of the Cinque Terre. Only the regular noisy slurping up of the train by the mountain reminds you of the modern world.

The action is at the harbor, where you'll find outdoor eateries ringing a humble piazza, a restaurant hanging on the edge of the castle, and a breakwater with a promenade, corralled by a natural amphitheater of terraced hills.

Join (or sit on a bench and watch) the locals devoting their leisure time to taking part in the *passeggiata*—lazily strolling together up and down the main street, doing *vasche* (laps). Learn—and live—the phrase *"la vita pigra di Vernazza"* (the lazy life of Vernazza).

Proud of their Vernazzan heritage, the town's residents like to brag: "Vernazza is locally owned. Portofino has sold out." Fearing change, keep-Vernazza-small proponents stopped the construction of a major road into the town and region. Families are tight and go back centuries; you'll notice certain surnames (such as Basso and Moggia) everywhere. In the winter, the population shrinks, as many people return to more-comfortable big-city apartments to spend the money they earned during the tourist season.

During the day in season the tiny harborfront and one main street are clogged with gawking group excursions. But early and late, Vernazza is the cool and content domain of locals...and travelers who are lucky enough to call the town home for a couple of nights.

Tourist Information

There's a park office at the train station (daily 8:30-19:30, shorter hours off-season). WCs are just down the platform.

Arrival in Vernazza

By Train: Vernazza's station is only about three train cars long, but the trains themselves are much longer, so most cars come to a stop in a long, dimly lit tunnel. Get out anyway, and walk through the tunnel and head for the light to reach the station. From there the main street flows through town right down to the harbor. If you're sleeping here, many locals who rent rooms will meet you at the station and walk you to your place (call ahead to tell them which train you're on).

By Car: Don't drive in Vernazza; the roads to town are in bad shape, and parking is mostly residents-only. If you're coming from the north, park in Levanto. If arriving from the south, park in La Spezia. From either town, hop on the train. (If you must drive here, leave your car at Parking Vernassoa, about a half-mile uphill from the top end of town; €15/day, free shuttle.)

Helpful Hints

Market: Vernazza's skimpy business community is augmented Tuesday mornings (8:00-13:00), when a meager gang of cars and trucks pulls into town for a tailgate market.

Baggage Storage: You can store your bags at the Cinque Terre Riviera agency on Via Roma (€5/bag, daily 9:30-18:30—see listing below).

Pharmacy: There's a little *farmacia* on the main drag, a few blocks up from the water (Via Roma 2, +39 0187 812 396).

Laundry: A small self-serve launderette is at the top of town next to the post office (Via Gavino 32, daily 8:00-20:00).

Booking Agency: Cinque Terre Riviera, run by Miriana, books vacation rentals in the Cinque Terre towns and La Spezia. They also store bags, sell tickets for Vernazza's summer opera, and can arrange transportation, cooking classes, and weddings (Via Roma 24, +39 351 785 8879).

Massage: Kate Allen offers a relaxing fusion of aromatic/Swedish/holistic massage and reflexology in her studio in the center across from the pharmacy (+39 0187 812 537, +39 333 568 4653).

Vernazza's pastel palette is chosen by a commissioner of good taste.

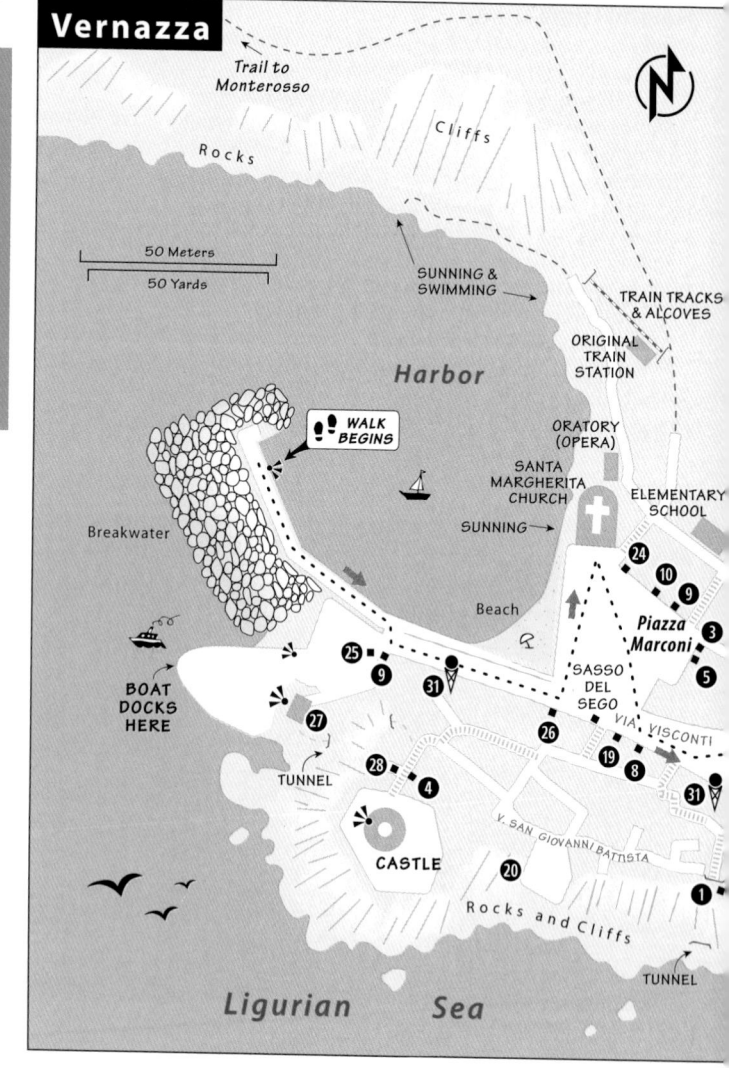

Vernazza

Trail to Monterosso

Cliffs

Rocks

50 Meters
50 Yards

SUNNING & SWIMMING

TRAIN TRACKS & ALCOVES

ORIGINAL TRAIN STATION

Harbor

WALK BEGINS

ORATORY (OPERA)

SANTA MARGHERITA CHURCH

ELEMENTARY SCHOOL

SUNNING

Breakwater

Beach

24
10
9

Piazza Marconi

3

25
9
31

SASSO DEL SEGO

5

BOAT DOCKS HERE

27

26

VIA VISCONTI

19
8

31

TUNNEL

28
4

V. SAN GIOVANNI BATTISTA

CASTLE

20

1

Rocks and Cliffs

TUNNEL

Ligurian   Sea

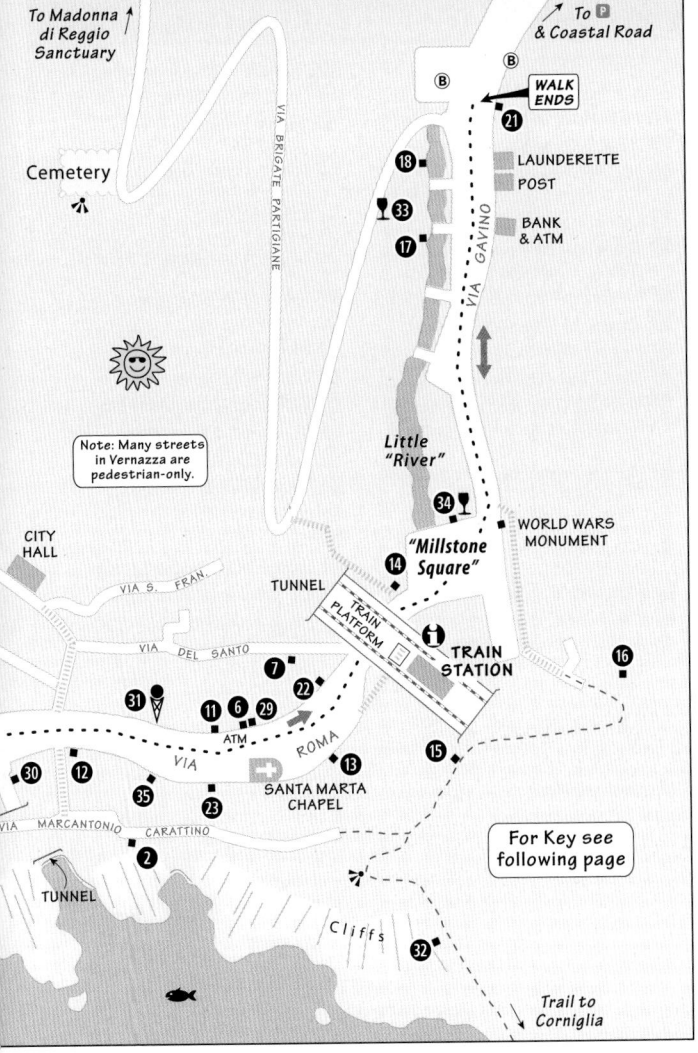

To Madonna di Reggio Sanctuary

To **P** & Coastal Road

B
B
WALK ENDS
21

LAUNDERETTE
POST

BANK & ATM

VIA BRIGATE PARTIGIANE

Cemetery

VIA GAVINO

Note: Many streets in Vernazza are pedestrian-only.

18
33
17

Little "River"

34

WORLD WARS MONUMENT

CITY HALL

"Millstone Square"

14

VIA S. FRAN.

TUNNEL

TRAIN PLATFORM

TRAIN STATION

VIA DEL SANTO

7
22
31
11 6 29
ATM

VIA
ROMA

16

30
12
35
23
13
15

SANTA MARTA CHAPEL

VIA MARCANTONIO CARATTINO

2

TUNNEL

For Key see following page

Cliffs

32

Trail to Corniglia

Vernazza Map Key

See map on previous page

Accommodations

1 La Malà & La Marina Rooms
2 Cinque Terre Vacation
3 Nicolina Rooms Reception & Ristorante Pizzeria Vulnetia
4 Monica Lercari Rooms
5 Francamaria Reception & Albergo Barbara Rooms
6 Vernazza Rentals
7 Vernazza Rooms Reception
8 Rosa Vitali Rooms
9 Maria Capellini Rooms (2)
10 Martina Callo Rooms, Capitano Rooms Reception & Trattoria del Capitano
11 Rooms Francesca Reception (Enoteca Sciacchetrà)
12 Ivo Basso Rooms
13 Eva's Rooms & Trattoria da Sandro
14 Manuela Moggia Rooms
15 Casa Cato
16 Giuliano Basso Rooms
17 Camere Fontanavecchia
18 La Rosa dei Venti
19 Gianni Franzi Reception/Ristorante
20 Gianni Franzi Rooms

Eateries & Other

21 Il Pirata delle Cinque Terre Café
22 Blue Marlin Bar
23 Lunch Box
24 Ananasso Bar
25 Ristorante Luca
26 Gambero Rosso
27 Ristorante Belforte
28 Ristorante al Castello
29 Antica Osteria il Baretto
30 Pizzeria da Ercole
31 Gelateria (3)
32 Bar la Torre
33 Cantina Cheo Wine Tasting
34 Cinque Sensi Wine Tasting
35 Cinque Terre Riviera Agency (Room Rental; Bag Storage; Opera Tickets)

VERNAZZA WALK

This self-guided walk gives you a quick overview of the town and starts out on its breakwater.

▶ *From the train station, walk downhill and all the way out onto the breakwater. Find a comfortable and safe place to sit and get to know Vernazza.*

The Town

The earliest references call the town "Fortress Vernazza." Its towers, fortified walls, and hillside terracing date mostly from the 12th through 15th century. Vernazza allied itself with the Republic of Genoa, a maritime power of the day. In the 12th century, the **big**

yellow central building facing the harbor was a site where Genoese warships were built.

In the Middle Ages, there was no beach or square. The water went right up to the buildings, where boats would tie up, Venetian-style. Imagine what Vernazza looked like in those days, when it was the biggest and richest of the Cinque Terre towns. The harborside buildings had a water gate (facing today's square) and a front door on the higher inland side. There was no pastel plaster—just fine stonework (traces of which survive above Trattoria del Capitano). The town, hiding behind its little bluff, was camouflaged by its gray stonework—certainly not gaily painted, lest it attract the eyes of marauding pirates. But apart from the added paint and plaster, the general shape and size of the town has changed little in five centuries.

Vernazza has two halves. *Sciuiu* (Vernazzan dialect for "flowery") is the sunny side on the left (with your back to the sea), and *luvegu* (dank) is the shady side on the right. Houses below the castle were connected by an interior arcade—ideal for fleeing attacks.

The "Ligurian pastel" colors of the buildings are regulated by the regional government's commissioner of good taste. The square before you is known for some of the area's finest restaurants.

While the town has 1,500 residents in summer, only 500 stay here through the winter. Vernazza has accommodations for about that many tourists.

Above Town

The small, **round tower** above the red building is another part of the city fortifications, recalling the town's importance in the Middle Ages. Back then, Genoa's enemies (rival maritime republics, especially Pisa) were Vernazza's enemies too. That tower recalls a time when the town was fortified by a stone wall.

Vineyards fill the mountainside beyond the town. Notice the many terraces. For six centuries, the economy was based on wine and olive oil. Then came the 1980s—and the tourists. Locals turned to tourism to make a living and stopped tending the land and vineyards.

Although many locals still maintain their small plots and proudly serve their family wines, the patchwork of vineyards is atomized and complex because of inheritance traditions. Historically, families divided their land among their children. Parents wanted each child to receive good land, though some lots were "kissed by the sun" while others were shady. Lots were split into increasingly tiny, unviable pieces, and many were eventually abandoned. The vineyards once stretched as high as you can see, but since fewer people sweat in the fields these days, the most distant terraces have gone wild again.

Church, School, and City Hall

Vernazza's Ligurian Gothic **church,** built with black stones quarried from Punta Mesco (the distant point between Monterosso and Levanto), dates from 1318. Note the gray stone (on the left) that marks the church's 16th-century expansion. The gray-and-red house above the spire is the **elementary school** (about 25 children attend). Older students go to the "big city," La Spezia. The red building on the hill to the right of the schoolhouse, a former monastery, is now the **City Hall.** Vernazza and neighboring Corniglia function as one community. Through most of the 1990s, the local government was Communist. In 1999, residents elected a coalition of many parties working to rise above ideologies and simply make Vernazza a better place. That practical notion of government continues here today.

Finally, on the top of the hill, with the best view of all, is the **town cemetery.** It's only fair that hardworking Vernazzans—who spend their lives climbing up and down and up and down and up and down the hillsides that hem in their little town—are rewarded with a world-class view from their eternal resting place.

▶ *Look high on your right to the castle.*

Castle (Castello Doria)

The castle, which is now just stones and a grassy park with super views, still guards the town (€2, daily 10:00-20:00, Nov-March weekends only; from the harbor, take the stairs by Trattoria Gianni and follow *Ristorante al Castello* signs—the tower is a few steps beyond). This was the town's watchtower back in pirate days.

In the squat tower below the castle, overlooking the water, Ristorante Belforte is a great spot for a glass of wine or a meal. From the breakwater you could follow the rope to the restaurant and pop inside, past an actual submarine door. A photo of a major storm showing the entire tower under a wave (not uncommon in the winter) hangs near the bar.

The squat Belforte tower (left) and castle tower (right) overlook the sea; both host restaurants.

Harbor

In a moderate storm, you'd get soaked where you're sitting, as waves routinely crash over the *molo* (**breakwater,** built in 1972). Waves can rearrange the huge rocks, depositing them from the breakwater onto the piazza and its benches. Freak waves have even washed away tourists squinting excitedly into their cameras. (I've seen it happen.) In 2007, an American woman was swept away and killed by a rogue wave.

The old **train line** (across the harbor) was constructed in 1874 to tie together a newly united Italy, linking Turin and Genoa with Rome. (The line now in use, hidden in a tunnel at this point, was built in the 1920s.) The yellow building alongside the tracks was Vernazza's **first train station.** Along the wall behind the tracks, you can see the four bricked-up alcoves where people once waited for trains. The wonderful concrete **sunbathing** strip (and place for late-night privacy) laid below the tracks along the rocks makes for a fun little stroll. (Buoys along the shoreline establish a boat-free swimming zone.)

Vernazza's **fishing fleet** is down to just a few boats with net spools, but Vernazzans are still more likely to own a boat than a car. Boats are moored on buoys, except in winter or when the red storm flag indicates rough seas (see the pole at the start of the breakwater). When the red flag flies, boat owners are permitted to pull them up onto the square—which is usually reserved for restaurant tables. In the 1970s, tiny Vernazza had one of Italy's top water polo teams, and the harbor was their "pool." Later, when the league required a real pool, Vernazza dropped out.

▶ *Stroll from the breakwater to the harbor square. Look for a small historic stone just before the narrow stairway on the right.*

Harbor Square (Piazza Marconi)

Vernazza, with the Cinque Terre's only natural harbor, was once the sole place boats could pick up the fine local wine. The two-foot-high square **stone** at the foot of the stairs is marked *Sasso del Sego* (stone of tallow). Workers crushed animal flesh and fat in its basin to make tallow, which drained out from the tiny hole below. The tallow was then used to waterproof boats or wine barrels.

Stonework is the soul of the region. Take some time to appreciate the medieval stonework and chestnut timbers of the restaurant interiors facing the harbor. From here steps lead to your right up to the castle.

Towns along this coast were designed as what's called a "Ligurian Palazzata"—an interlinked series of buildings intended to provide protection from seaborne attacks. Vernazza's harborfront retains its thousand-year-old "stockade" of buildings, connected with tiny and easy-to-defend staircases leading from the vulnerable harbor higher into the community.

▶ *Cross to the church side of the harbor, and peek into the tiny street leading away from the water with its commotion of arches. Vernazza's most characteristic **side streets** (caruggi) lead up from here. Another*

Colorful boats ashore on Vernazza's harbor beach

narrow set of stairs marks the beginning of the trail that leads up, up, up to the iconic view of Vernazza—and on to Monterosso.

Vernazza's Church

Vernazza's harborfront **church** sits on the tiny piazza, decorated with a river-rock mosaic. This popular hangout spot is where the town's older ladies soak up the last bit of sun, and kids enjoy a level patch for playing ball. The church, nestled awkwardly into the rocks, is unusual for its east-facing (rather than the standard west-facing) entryway. With relative peace and prosperity in the 16th century, the townspeople doubled the size of their church, extending it west over what was the little piazza that faced it.

Enter under a statue of St. Margaret, patron saint of Vernazza, and climb the steps into the nave. The space was originally dark (with just the upper slit windows) before the bigger gothic windows were added with the 16th-century expansion. The lighter pillars in the back mark the extension. Three historic portable crosses hanging on the walls are carried through town during religious processions. These are replicas of crosses that (locals like to believe) Vernazzan ships once carried on crusades to the Holy Land.

▶ *Now walk back across the harbor square and head left into town. On the main drag, continue uphill to...*

Vernazza's "Main Street"

You're now strolling through Vernazza's "commercial center": souvenir shops, wine shops, the Blue Marlin Bar (a good nightspot), and so on. You'll walk by a *gelateria*, bakery, pharmacy, grocery, and another *gelateria*. There are plenty of fun and cheap food-to-go options here.

Stop by Vernazza's tranquil church...

...and stroll its irresistible main street.

The small stone chapel with iron grillwork over the window (on the right) is the tiny **Chapel of Santa Marta,** where Mass is celebrated on special Sundays. While it's easy to get distracted by all the tourists, try to see through them to notice locals going about their business.

▶ *Pause just before the train tracks.*

Vernazza is built around this one street, which is basically a lid over the stream in its ravine. During torrential rainstorms, the surrounding hills act like a funnel, directing flash-flood waters and mudslides right through the middle of town. That's precisely what happened in the devastating flood of October 25, 2011. Four townspeople lost their lives. Imagine this street, from here to the harbor, buried under 13 feet of mud. Every shop, restaurant, and hotel on the main drag had to be rewired, replumbed, and re-equipped.

The second set of train tracks (nearer the harbor) has been renovated to lessen disruptive noise. At the base of the stairs a handy monitor displays up-to-the-minute schedules for arriving and departing trains (including any running late—*ritardo*). The walls under the tracks serve as a sort of community information center. Just above the tracks (to the right), the town provides limited space for political advertising (but only during the weeks leading up to an election).

▶ *Hike a few steps under and above the tracks to the little square.*

"Millstone Square"

The **millstones** set on the square are a reminder that Vernazza's water mill was once powered by the town stream (which runs underground here; you've been walking over it since leaving the harbor area). You can still see the tiny "river" if you follow this road up a few steps. Until the 1950s, the river ran openly through the center of town. Old-timers recall the days before the breakwater, when the river cascaded down, charming bridges spanned the ravine, and the surf sent waves rolling up Vernazza's main drag.

Corralling this stream under the modern street, and forcing it to take a hard turn here, contributed to the damage caused by the 2011 flood. As a result, Swiss engineers redesigned the drainage system, so any future floods will be less destructive. Nets installed above the town now protect it from landslides.

On the wall ahead, at the bend in the road, notice the **World Wars Monument**—dedicated to those killed in World Wars I and II. Not a family in Vernazza was spared.

The **path to Corniglia** begins from here (behind and above the monument). Even if you don't plan to hike its entire length, you don't have to go far to find fine views over Vernazza's stony peninsula.

▶ *To see a more workaday part of Vernazza, head a couple of minutes uphill from here to the...*

Top of Town

First you'll pass the **ambulance barn** (on the left, at #7, with big brown garage doors and a *croce verde Vernazza* sign), where a group of volunteers is always on call for a dash to the hospital, 40 minutes away in La Spezia. Farther up, you'll come to a functional strip of modern apartment blocks facing the river. In this practical zone—the only place in town that allows cars—are a bank, the post office, a launderette, and the popular bar/café called Il Pirata delle Cinque Terre. A parking lot fills the square called **Fontana Vecchia,** named for an "old fountain" that's so old, it's long gone. Shuttle buses run from here to hamlets and sanctuaries in the hills above.

Looming over this neighborhood is a terraced hill capped by the town cemetery (a 20-minute steep hike from here) and, a 30-minute climb beyond that, the town's Madonna di Reggio sanctuary.

EXPERIENCES IN VERNAZZA

Hikes from Vernazza

For a rundown of ambitious hikes from Vernazza—including the main coastal trail to Corniglia and to Monterosso—see page 24. The following shorter alternatives closer to town offer classic photo ops. They are steeply, but briefly, uphill (about 10 minutes to the best views and park ticket checkpoints).

For the best light in the morning, follow the trail **toward Corniglia;** you'll twist up through vineyards to earn great views down over the stony back side of Vernazza's peninsula, with its round castle tower poking up and a Monterosso backdrop. The best views are from just before the national park ticket checkpoint. If you need a rewarding rest up here, Bar la Torre offers drinks with a grand view.

The trail **toward Monterosso** has the best light in the evening. From the harbor, you'll hike up through the steep and narrow alleys before popping out on the trail above town. Follow this around the bluff,

You can hike uphill from Vernazza (toward Corniglia or Monterosso) for classic views.

enjoying increasingly better views of Vernazza's tidy pastel harbor. The views are fine before the ticket booth, but even better after—if you don't want to buy a Cinque Terre park card, you can hike up here in the evening, after the park officially closes (typically around 19:00).

Hike to the Cemetery: To hike up to Vernazza's sweet little **cemetery,** find the steep lane from the ravine at the top of town. From here it's a 20-minute hike to the top. You'll find a peaceful world of lovingly tended family graves with stunning views over the Cinque Terre. Imagine the entire village sadly trudging up here during funerals. The cemetery is peaceful and evocative at sunset, when the fading light touches each crypt.

▲▲Madonna di Reggio Shuttle Bus Joyride and/or Hike

For a cheap and scenic joyride (50 minutes, €1.50) with friendly drivers, ride the ATC shuttle bus, which loops about four times a day from the top of Vernazza to sanctuaries and hamlets high in the hills and back (check schedule posted at the bus stop, ask at the TI, or check online at www.atcesercizio.it). Look for the bus serving Madonna di Reggio and Fornacchi. Stay on for the full loop back to Vernazza, or get off at Madonna di Reggio and return downhill on foot.

Joyride: The bus ride is absolutely stunning, though it can be crowded. As you ride, you'll see tiny hamlets and hillside terraces that go back a thousand years. You'll switchback past chestnut trees, which historically provided wood for fuel and lumber, and chestnuts, which were ground to make a kind of flour in a land with no grain.

Hiking Down from Madonna di Reggio: For a delightful and easy (if steep) half-hour hike into Vernazza, ask the driver to let you out at the stop for Vernazza's sanctuary, Madonna di Reggio.

First, walk two minutes below the bus stop to the sanctuary, which dates from 1248 and has a Romanesque facade. Inside the church, votives (little ships and paintings of ships in angry seas given as tokens of thanks) fill the rear corner—gifts from sailors who survived storms and soldiers who survived wars. A volunteer staffs the church selling coffee, water, and snacks.

From here signs direct you to trail #508—the historic trail down to Vernazza. You'll be walking on thousand-year-old cobbles through abandoned olive groves and past the Stations of the Cross, which have inspired generations of processions trudging up from Vernazza. You may see a parked *trenino,* a minitrain that helps farmers get their grapes from distant fields to their trucks.

You'll descend through the cemetery, then either take the stairs down to the train station or continue to the left down the lane to the square called Fontana Vecchia, where you caught the shuttle bus.

Beaches

The harbor's sandy cove has sunning rocks and showers by the breakwater. The sunbathing lane directly under the church has a shower. A ladder on the seaside of the breakwater aids deep-water swimmers.

Boat Rides

In addition to the regularly scheduled big boats that depart from Vernazza's harbor (see page 18), hiring your own boat can be handy for intertown transport. It's also a great way to escape the crowds and get a different angle on the Cinque Terre splendor. From Vernazza, figure around €50 one-way to sail to the other towns (for up to six passengers in an outboard). Or hire a boat for a one-hour sightseeing cruise of the

Enjoy one of several hikes from Vernazza...

...and the sunning rocks at the harbor.

entire Cinque Terre (about €150); one popular stop is the tiny *acqua pendente* (waterfall) cove between Vernazza and Monterosso, which locals call their *laguna blu*.

Some boat captains offer evening *aperitivo* cruises. At Vernazza's breakwater you'll find **Nord Est,** run by Vincenzo (with help from Cesare), the best-established option (+39 338 700 0436, www.nordest-vernazza.it). **Vernazza Water Taxi,** run by Pietro, is another choice (+39 338 911 3869, www.vernazzawatertaxi.it).

Wine Tasting

Cantina Cheo, above the train station near the top of town, invites you in for afternoon tastings of its own wines—grown on the nearby hillside (€5, more for private tours, April-mid-Oct daily 14:30-18:30, closed off-season, Via Brigate Partigiane 1, +39 333 959 4758, www.cheo.it). Cinque Sensi, behind the train station, offers an assortment of wines with snacks (€15-25, Via Roma 71, daily 12:00-24:00, +39 338 766 7423).

NIGHTLIFE IN VERNAZZA

A Little Taste of Opera: In summer, a pair of talented opera singers comes to Vernazza once or twice a week to perform with piano accompaniment in the town's small oratory, a medieval building with fine acoustics (just up the steps from the church). Performances begin at 19:00 and last just over an hour—strategically timed to squeeze between a late-afternoon aperitivo on the harbor and a 20:30 dinner reservation (€25, June-mid-Oct Wed and Fri, April-May Fri only, book tickets at Cinque Terre Riviera office on the main street—see "Helpful Hints," earlier).

The Bar Scene: Vernazza's nightlife centers on the bars on its waterfront piazza and generally shuts down pretty early (nightspots are required to close by midnight). The **Blue Marlin Bar** dominates the scene with a mix of locals and tourists, good drinks, and an open piano. If you play piano, you're welcome to join in. **Ananasso Bar** offers early-evening happy-hour fun and cocktails (*aperitivi*) that both locals and visitors enjoy. Its harborfront tables get the last sunshine of the day. For more on these bars, see their listings under "Eating in Vernazza," later.

Vernazza's breakwater offers a shimmering view of the harbor at night.

SLEEPING IN VERNAZZA

Vernazza lacks any real hotels, and almost all of my listings are *affitta-camere* (private rooms for rent). I favor hosts who rent multiple rooms and have a proven track record of good communication (they speak just enough English, have email, and are reliable). Airbnb is really big in Vernazza.

Most places accept only cash, promise free Wi-Fi (often spotty), and don't include breakfast unless noted. Some have killer views, and some come with lots of stairs. Expect noise at night: trains tearing through, church bells (7:00-22:00), crashing waves, delivery vans in the upper town. Come to think of it, just pack earplugs.

Some places have all their beds in one building; others have rooms scattered all over town. Some have an informal reception desk (often at a restaurant or other business) where you can check in; others have no reception at all. The Vernazza map in this book shows only the places that have a fixed address or reception office; if I mention "reception," you'll check in there.

If you overnight here, communicate your arrival time to your host and get clear instructions on where to meet and pick up the keys.

They'll usually offer to meet you at the train station if they know when you're coming.

Rooms For Rent (*Affittacamere*)

The **Cinque Terre Riviera** agency, based in Vernazza, rents rooms here and throughout the region (see page 57).

Scattered Through the Town Center

More Expensive, with More Amenities

$$$$ La Malà is the town's jet-setter pad. Four crisp, pristine white rooms boast fancy hotel-type extras and a shared seaview terrace. It's a climb—way up to the top of town—but they'll carry your bags to and from the station. Book early; this place fills up quickly (includes breakfast at a bar, family rooms, air-con, +39 334 287 5718, www.lamala.it, info@ lamala.it, charming Giamba and his mama, Armanda). They also rent two rooms at the simpler **$ "Armanda's Room"** nearby—a great value, since you get Giamba's attention to detail and amenities without paying for a big view (includes simple breakfast, air-con, www.armanda.it).

$$$$ Cinque Terre Vacation rents two luxury apartments (1- and 2-bedroom, sleeping up to 6) that overlook the sea and town from private, spacious terraces. The light-filled, airy units come with sea breezes and a crashing-waves soundtrack. The apartments can be connected for even larger groups (air-con, fully equipped kitchens, 2-night minimum, climb steps up to Via Carattino 12 or Via Mazzini 17, +39 345 363 6118, www.cinqueterrevacation.com, ruth@cinqueterrevacation.com, run by helpful American-Italian Ruth and her family).

$$$ Nicolina Rooms consists of five rooms and two apartments in three buildings. Two cheaper rooms are in the center over the pharmacy, up a few steep steps; another, pricier studio with a terrace is on a twisty lane above the harbor; and four more rooms are in a building beyond the church, with great views and church bells (all include breakfast, Piazza Marconi 29—check in at Pizzeria Vulnetia, +39 0187 821 193, +39 333 842 6879, www.camerenicolina.it, info@ camerenicolina.it).

$$$ La Marina Rooms is run by hardworking Cristian, who speaks English and happily carries bags to and from the station. He rents a single, two doubles, and two apartments, all well-tended, airy, and renovated, most high above the main street, and most with sea views and air-con (+39 338 476 7472, www.lamarinarooms.com, mapcri@yahoo.it).

$$$ Monica Lercari rents several rooms with modern comforts, including one (more expensive) perched at the top of town with a seaview terrace (air-con, +39 0187 812 296, mobile +39 320 025 4515, monimarimax@gmail.com). Monica and her husband, Massimo, run the recommended Ristorante al Castello.

Simpler, Good-Value Places

$$ Francamaria and her husband, Andrea, rent 10 sharp, comfortable, and creatively renovated rooms near the harbor square, with relatively few stairs (family rooms, air-con, reception desk on the ground floor at Piazza Marconi 30, +39 328 711 9728, www.francamaria.com, francamariareservation@gmail.com). They also rent a room in Manarola.

$$ Vernazza Rentals offers several rooms, including a spacious and classy room on the harbor square, and a *molto chic* split-level apartment on a quiet side street (reception at Via Roma 27, +39 339 834 2486, mobile +39 338 117 6814, www.vernazzarentals.com, info@vernazzarentals.com).

$$ Vernazza Rooms, run by Massimo, rents 14 rooms: Four are above the Blue Marlin Bar looking down on the main street, and seven are a steep climb higher up, just under the City Hall (big family apartments, a few with air-con and others with fans, fridges in all rooms, arrange check-in time in advance and meet your host at Via del Santo 9, +39 351 918 3164, www.vernazzarooms.com, info@vernazzarooms.com).

$$ Lovely Rosa Vitali rents a four-person apartment with a kitchen; it's across from the pharmacy overlooking the main street—and beyond the worst of the train noise (ring bell at Via Visconti 10—just before the tobacco shop near Piazza Marconi, +39 340 267 5009, www.rosacamere.it, rosa.vitali@libero.it).

$$ Maria Capellini rents two simple, clean rooms that face each other across the harbor. One is at ground level just steps from the beach, with a view; the other looks over a skinny street (fridge, fans, +39 347 441 3695, www.mariacapellini.com, mariacapellini@hotmail.it, kindly Maria and Giacomo, and son Gianni).

$$ Martina Callo's four old-fashioned, spartan rooms overlook the harbor square; they're up plenty of steps near the silent-at-night church tower. Two rooms have a sea view and cost more (family room, air-con in most rooms, ring bell at Piazza Marconi 26, +39 0187 812

365, mobile +39 329 435 5344, www.roomartina.it, roomartina@roomartina.it, Martina and her father, Giuseppe).

$$ Albergo Barbara rents eight tidy, Ikea-chic top-floor rooms overlooking the square with an attic communal lounge. Most have small windows and small views; view rooms are more expensive. It's a good value in a nice location, run by Alessio and Alberto (cheaper rooms with shared bathroom, lots of stairs, reserve online with credit card but pay cash, Piazza Marconi 30, +39 0187 812 398, www.albergobarbara.it, info@albergobarbara.it).

$ Rooms Francesca offers one tidy room with sea views and air-con, and a two-bedroom apartment with fans. Both hide out in the steep streets just below City Hall (check in at Enoteca Sciacchetrà at Via Roma 19, +39 0187 821 112, mobile +39 339 191 2962, www.5terre-vernazza.it, moggia.franco@libero.it; Francesca and Franco).

$ Ivo Basso rents two tight but well-appointed rooms several flights of stairs above the main street (air-con, Via Roma 6, +39 333 477 5521, www.ivocamere.com, post@ivocamere.com).

More Options

If my recommendations above are full, try these:

$$ Capitano Rooms (3 rooms and 1 apartment several flights of stairs above main drag, fans; ask for Julia, Paolo, Edoardo, or Barbara at Trattoria del Capitano restaurant on the main square at Piazza Marconi 21, +39 0187 812 201, www.tavernavernazza.com, info@tavernavernazza.com); **$$ Eva's Rooms** (a single and a double on the main street, air-con, train noise, 2-night minimum, +39 334 798 6500 or +39 331 153 2035, www.evasrooms.it, evasrooms@yahoo.it, Rebecca and Maurizia); **$$$ Manuela Moggia** (3 apartments and 2 rooms, behind train station at Via Gavino 22 and on main square, +39 0187 812 397, mobile +39 333 413 6374, www.manuela-vernazza.com, info@manuela-vernazza.com).

In the Inland Part of Town

Above the Train Station: $$$$ Casa Cato offers five modern, tight but well-outfitted rooms, three with private balconies and two with a shared balcony, all overlooking the sea and town (RS%, air-con, fridge, expect some train noise, +39 334 123 8579, www.casacatocinqueterre.com, info@casacatocinqueterre.com, Lisa). They also rent an apartment in the center of town.

$$ Giuliano Basso's four carefully crafted, well-appointed rooms form a cozy little compound with a common lounge and view terrace, straddling a ravine among orange trees. Giuliano—the town's last stone-layer—proudly built the place himself. To reach this quiet retreat on the green hillside just above town and the train station, you'll climb part-way up the Corniglia footpath (2 rooms have air-con, more train noise than others; follow the main road up above the station, take the ramp up toward Corniglia just before Pensione Sorriso, follow the path, and watch for a sharp left turn—or ask Giuliano to meet you at the station; +39 333 341 4792, www.cameregiuliano.com, giuliano@cdh.it).

In the Ravine at the Top of Town: These practical options are a five-minute, gently uphill stroll behind the train station. While this functional zone is less atmospheric, it is easy to access (with fewer steep stairs). There's no train or church-bell noise—the constant soundtrack is Vernazza's gurgling river—but there can be traffic noise.

$$ Camere Fontanavecchia, run by Annamaria, is the best choice here, with eight bright and cheery rooms (three with terraces) overlooking the ravine and its rushing river (Via Gavino 15, +39 333 454 9371, www.cinqueterrecamere.com, m.annamaria@libero.it). She also rents an apartment.

$ La Rosa dei Venti ("The Compass Rose"), run by Giuliana Basso, houses three airy, good-value rooms in her childhood home, on the third floor of an apartment building (call to arrange meeting time, air-con, Via Gavino 19, mobile +39 333 762 4679, www.larosadeiventi-vernazza.it, info@larosadeiventi-vernazza.it).

Guesthouse (Pensione)

$$$ Gianni Franzi, who owns a busy restaurant on the harbor square, runs the closest thing to a hotel in Vernazza. His 24 small rooms are in three buildings a hundred tight, winding stairs above the harbor square. Some rooms are funky and decorated à la shipwreck, with tiny balconies and grand sea views. The comfy, newer rooms lack views. All guests have access to a super-scenic cliff-hanging garden and panoramic terrace (where breakfast is served in season). Pick up your keys at the restaurant, but on Wednesday, when the restaurant is closed, call ahead to make other arrangements (RS%, closed Jan-Feb, Piazza Marconi 1, +39 0187 812 228, mobile +39 393 9008 155, www.giannifranzi.it, info@giannifranzi.it, Emanuele and Simona).

Breakfast

Vernazza has plenty of options, from full bacon and eggs (Blue Marlin and Capitano), to fresh pastries from a Sicilian bakery (Il Pirata), to coffee and a sweet roll on the harborfront (Ananasso), to any number of bakeries selling sweet and savory options to go. Here are your main options from the top of town to the harbor.

$ Il Pirata delle Cinque Terre, at the parking lot at the top of town, is playful, efficient, and comfortable, and serves tasty breakfast bruschetta, frittatas, and an array of fresh pastries. The fun service of the dynamic duo Gianluca and Massimo (hardworking Sicilian twins, a.k.a. the Cannoli brothers) makes up for the lack of a view. They pride themselves on not serving bacon and eggs, since "this is Italy" (Fri-Wed 7:00-24:00, closed Thu, also serves lunch and dinner—see later, Via Gavino 36, +39 0187 812 047).

$$ Blue Marlin Bar (midtown, just below the train station) serves a good array of clearly priced à la carte breakfast items (Italian breakfast from 7:00, eggs and bacon 8:30-11:30). If you're awaiting a train and the platform isn't crowded, it's pleasant to have a drink at Blue Marlin's outdoor seating in view of the tracks (Thu-Tue 7:00-23:00, closed Wed).

$ Lunch Box is the hardworking new kid on the block, with lots of hot options and a fun little perch for a couple of tables overlooking the main drag (daily 7:00-22:00, also serves lunch and dinner—see later, Via Roma 34, +39 338 908 2841, Stefano).

$$ Trattoria del Capitano offers outdoor seating on the harbor, as well as cozy spots inside the restaurant and a full menu (Wed-Mon 8:00-22:00, closed Tue, on Piazza Marconi, +39 0187 812 201, hardworking Paolo and Barbara speak English).

$$ Ananasso Bar has a youthful energy, a great location right on the harbor, and a skimpy Italian breakfast menu (toasted *panini,* pastries, Muesli with yogurt, and cappuccino). You can eat a bit cheaper at the bar (you're welcome to picnic on the nearby bench or seawall rocks with a sea view) or enjoy the best-situated tables in town (Fri-Wed 8:00-late, closed Thu, on Piazza Marconi).

Picnic Breakfast: Drop by one of Vernazza's many little bakeries, focaccia shops, or grocery stores to assemble a breakfast to eat on the breakwater. Top it off with a coffee in a nearby bar.

Twin brothers run the popular Il Pirata delle Cinque Terre café.

Lunch and Dinner

Vernazza's restaurants work hard to win your business. Wander around at about 20:00 and compare the ambience. If you dine in Vernazza but are staying in another town, check train schedules before sitting down to eat, as evening trains run less frequently, with gaps in the schedule. To get an outdoor table on summer weekends, reserve ahead. Harborside restaurants and bars are easygoing. You're welcome to grab a cup of coffee or glass of wine and disappear somewhere on the breakwater, returning your glass when you're done.

Harborside

$$$ Gianni Franzi is an old standby for well-prepared seafood and pastas. Emanuele, Lorenzo, and their crew provide steady, reliable, and friendly service. The outdoor seating is partially tucked under an arcade, while the indoor setting is big, open, and classy. The *cucina tipica Vernazza* page of their menu showcases local specialties (Thu-Tue 12:00-15:00 & 19:00-22:00, closed Wed, +39 0187 812 228).

    $$ Trattoria del Capitano feels unpretentious and serves a short menu of straightforward local dishes, including *spaghetti allo* *scoglio*—pasta entangled with various types of seafood (for hours and location, see "Breakfast," earlier).

$$$ Ristorante Pizzeria Vulnetia has a nautical, jovial atmosphere and is proud of its locally sourced ingredients. Unlike the others, it also dishes up thin-crust pizzas—making this a good choice for a group with differing tastes, those on a budget, and families (Tue-Sun 12:00-22:00, closed Mon, Piazza Marconi 29, +39 0187 821 193, Tullio and Federica).

$$$ Ristorante Luca serves seafood dishes at a roofed-over circle of tables right on the breakwater—a memorable spot (Sat-Thu 11:30-22:00, closed Fri, +39 0187 812 113, Luca and Andrea).

$$$$ Gambero Rosso rounds out the options on the harbor. Long the top restaurant in town, today it's lost its edge (it was sold to a big-city restaurateur who runs it from afar). Still, it's reliably good, and has a fine interior and great outdoor tables (Fri-Wed 12:00-15:00 & 19:00-22:00, closed Thu and Dec-Feb, Piazza Marconi 7, +39 0187 812 265).

Above the Harbor, by the Castle

$$$$ Ristorante Belforte is a cut above the rest, serving a fine blend of traditional and creative cuisine, fishy *spaghetti alla Bruno*, *trofie al pesto* (hand-rolled noodles with pesto), and classic *antipasto misto di pesce*—an assortment of fish on five small plates (€25/person; 2-person minimum). Enter from the breakwater; a rope leads up stairs to a web of tables embedded in four levels of the old castle. While their indoor seating is great, for the ultimate seaside perch, reserve a table on the *terrazza con vista* (view terrace) or request the "lovers' table" on its own little terrace. Most of Belforte's seating is outdoors—if the weather's bad, the interior can get crowded. Late in the evening, Andrea cranks up the fun (Wed-Mon 12:00-15:00 & 19:00-22:00, closed Tue and Nov-March, +39 0187 812 222, Michela).

$$$ Ristorante al Castello is a homey seafood restaurant on a covered terrace just below the castle, with commanding views out to sea (to reward your climb). It's run by gracious, English-speaking Monica and her husband, Massimo, who are proud of their €30 mixed grilled-fish plate (which two or even three can split) and their *trofie al pesto*. Reserve one of the dozen romantic cliffside seaview tables for two—some of the tables snake around the castle, where you'll feel like you're eating all alone with the Mediterranean. Monica offers a free *sciacchetrà* or *limoncello* with biscotti with this book by request

(Thu-Tue 12:00-15:00 & 19:00-22:00, closed Wed and Nov-April, +39 0187 812 296).

Near the Train Station

These places have no harbor ambience but are pleasing and slightly cheaper.

$$ Trattoria da Sandro, on the main drag, mixes quality Genovese and Ligurian cuisine with friendly service and can be a peaceful alternative to the harborside scene. The family proudly maintains its cultural traditions and dishes up award-winning stuffed mussels (Wed-Mon 12:00-15:30 & 18:30-22:00, closed Tue, Via Roma 62, +39 0187 812 223, Argentina and Alessandro).

$$ Antica Osteria il Baretto is another solid bet for homey, reasonably priced traditional cuisine, run by Simone and Jenny. As it's off the harbor and less glitzy than the others, it's favored by locals who prefer less noisy English while they eat great homemade fare. Sitting deep in their interior can be a tranquil escape (Tue-Sun 12:00-22:00, closed Mon, indoor and outdoor seating in summer, Via Roma 31, +39 0187 812 381).

Other Eating Options

$$ Blue Marlin Bar, on the main street, busts out of the Vernazzan cuisine rut with a short, creative menu of more casual dishes (pizzas, salads). It's a good choice if you want to grab something basic rather than dine (for more details and hours, see "Breakfast," earlier).

$$ Il Pirata delle Cinque Terre, a huge hit for breakfast, also attracts travelers for lunch and dinner. Even though you're eating facing a parking lot, the food, service, and energy are great. And many are charmed by the Cannoli twins, who entertain while they serve. The menu (pastas and salads) is aimed squarely at American tourists' taste buds (lunch from 12:00, reserve ahead for dinner from 18:00, good cannoli and Sicilian slushies, at the top of town; for more details and contact info, see "Breakfast," earlier). The self-serve laundry is next door for those who like to multitask.

$ Lunch Box serves *panini,* salads, and fresh fruit juices from a clever and flexible menu. Assemble your own salad (or juice) from a long list of ingredients (for hours and location, see "Breakfast," earlier).

$ Pizzeria da Ercole dishes out pies cheap and fast on simple tables right in the busy center of town (or to take away). More tables are in a humble little secret terrace hiding in the back, where tour guides go to escape their groups (daily, Via Visconti 34, +39 338 771 3844).

Pizzerias, Sandwiches, and Groceries: Vernazza's main-street eateries offer a fine range of quick meals. Several bakeries and creative little takeaway joints sell sandwiches and pizza by the slice. **Pino's grocery store** at Via Visconti 19 makes inexpensive sandwiches to order (daily 8:00-13:00 & 17:00-19:30 except closed Sun evening). There's a **Co-op** grocery at Via Roma 39 (next to the Blue Marlin Bar).

Gelato: The town has plenty of good gelato shops. On the harbor, the aptly named **Gelateria Il Porticciolo** ("Marina") uses fresh ingredients to create intense flavors (try their *cannella*—cinnamon, or *nocciola*—hazelnut). **Gelateria Vernazza,** near the top of the main street, takes its gelato seriously, occasionally flirting with creative ingredients (soy) and flavors (*riso*—rice, and ricotta and fig). **Gelateria Amore Mio** (midtown) used to be Gelateria Stalin, founded in 1968 by a pastry chef with that unfortunate name; now it's run by his niece Sonia and nephew Francesco, with great people-watching tables.

Corniglia

If you think of the Cinque Terre as the Beatles, Corniglia is Ringo. This tiny, sleepy town is the only one of the five not directly on the water. According to legend, the town was originally settled by a Roman farmer who named it for his mother, Cornelia (which is how Corniglia is pronounced). Locals claim that its ancient residents produced a wine so widely exported that vases have been found at Pompeii stamped with the town name. Wine remains Corniglia's lifeblood today. Sample some when you're in town.

Less visited than the other Cinque Terre towns, Corniglia has fewer tourists, cooler temperatures, a laid-back main square, a few restaurants, a windy overlook on its promontory, and plenty of private rooms for rent. You don't go to Corniglia for the beach: Its once fine beach below the station has washed away. From the town center, signs for *al mare* or *Marina* point to where a stepped path leads steeply down to sunning rocks.

ORIENTATION TO CORNIGLIA

Hill-capping Corniglia is connected with its train station far below by a long set of stairs, and much easier by a hardworking little shuttle bus. Its reliable schedule is posted both at the station and in the town. Because of the steep distance between the town and its station, and the lack of a boat dock, Corniglia is inconvenient as a home base for town-hopping.

Tourist Information

A park information office is down at the train station (daily 8:30-18:30, shorter hours off-season). At busy times there may also be a kiosk up in town on Ciappà square.

Arrival in Corniglia

By Train: From the station far below town, a footpath zigzags up 385 steps to the town in about 20 minutes. Or hop on the tiny ATC shuttle that connects the station with Corniglia's Ciappà square, where my short self-guided walk starts (€1.50, buy tickets at park office—€2.50

Nearly 400 steps link Corniglia's town (above) to its train station (below).

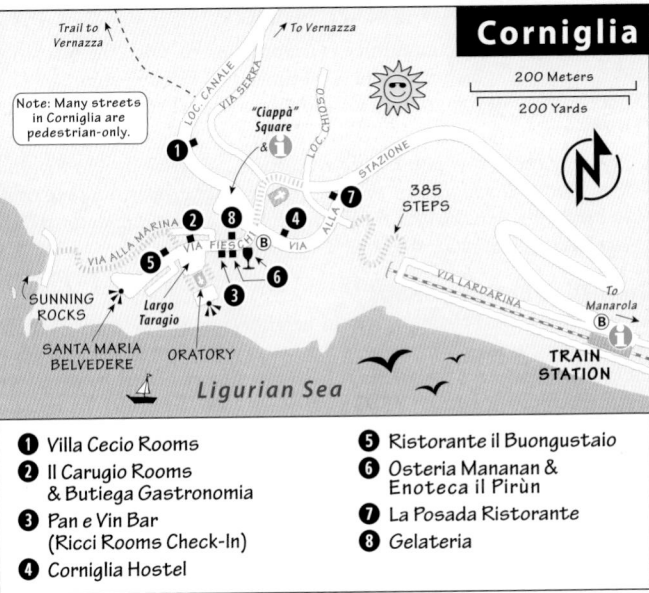

Corniglia

Note: Many streets in Corniglia are pedestrian-only.

Trail to Vernazza

To Vernazza

LOC. CANALE

VIA SERRA

"Ciappà" Square & ℹ️

LOC. CHIOSO

VIA ALLA STAZIONE

200 Meters
200 Yards

385 STEPS

VIA ALLA MARINA

VIA FIESCA

VIA

VIA LARDARINA

To Manarola

SUNNING ROCKS

Largo Taragio

SANTA MARIA BELVEDERE

ORATORY

Ligurian Sea

TRAIN STATION

❶ Villa Cecio Rooms
❷ Il Carugio Rooms & Butiega Gastronomia
❸ Pan e Vin Bar (Ricci Rooms Check-In)
❹ Corniglia Hostel
❺ Ristorante il Buongustaio
❻ Osteria Mananan & Enoteca il Pirùn
❼ La Posada Ristorante
❽ Gelateria

from driver, covered by park passes; departs about every 15 minutes from 8:00-20:00, buses fill quickly).

If leaving Corniglia by train, either walk down or review the shuttle schedule to plan your return to the station.

By Car: Only residents can park on the main road between the recommended Villa Cecio and the point where the steep switchback staircase meets the road. Beyond that area, anyone can park for a fee. All parking areas are within an easy and fairly level walk from the town center.

CORNIGLIA WALK

We'll explore this tiny town—population 240—and end at a scenic viewpoint. This self-guided walk might take 30 minutes or more...but only if you let yourself browse, sample the wine, or lick gelato.

▶ Begin at the upper shuttle bus stop, on...

Ciappà Square

The gateway to this community is Ciappà square, with the bus stop, an ATM, an old wine press, and sometimes a TI kiosk in summer. The Cinque Terre's designation as a national park sparked a revitalization of the town.

▸ *Look for the arrow pointing to the centro. Stroll along Via Fieschi, the spine of Corniglia. In the fall, the smell of grapes (on their way to becoming wine) wafts from busy cellars. Along this main street, you'll see…*

Corniglia's Enticing Shops

As you enter Via Fieschi, a trio of neighboring gelato shops jockeys for your business. My favorite is the last one you come to (at #74, on the right), **Alberto's Gelateria** (open late). Before ordering, get a free taste of Alberto's *miele di Corniglia,* made from local honey; he and Cristina are also proud of their basil flavor. Their lemon slush (*granita*) takes pucker to new heights.

Farther along, located in a cool cantina on the left, **Enoteca il Pirùn** is named for a type of oddly shaped old-fashioned wine pitcher designed to aerate the wine and give the alcohol more kick as you squirt it into your mouth (Via Fieschi 115). Try some local wines (small tastes generally free, €3/glass). If you order wine to drink from the *pirùn,* Mario will give you a bib. While this is a practicality (rookies tend to dribble), it also makes a nice souvenir.

Keep walking and you'll pass **Butiega** Gastronomia (#142), an old-fashioned grocery store/deli where Simone sells organic local specialties (daily 8:00-20:00). For picnickers, they offer made-to-order ham-and-cheese sandwiches and a fun *antipasti misti* (priced

Corniglia's lanes offer slice-of-life scenes…

…and enticing, authentic shops.

by weight). He also prepares pesto and other specialties daily in the shop's tiny kitchen. You'll find good places to picnic farther along on this walk.

▶ *Following Via Fieschi, you'll end up at the mellow...*

Main Square (Largo Taragio)

On the main square, tables from two bars and a trattoria spill around a WWI memorial and the town's old well. It once piped in natural spring water from the hillside to locals living without plumbing. What looks like a church is the **Oratory of Santa Caterina.** (An oratory is a kind of spiritual clubhouse for a service group doing social work in the name of the Catholic Church.) Up the stairs and behind the oratory you'll find a terrace that children have made into a soccer field. The stone benches and viewpoint make this a peaceful place for a picnic (less crowded than the end-of-town viewpoint, described next).

Opposite the oratory, notice how steep steps lead down Via alla Marina, taking you in five minutes to sunning rocks and a small deck (with a shower and treacherous entry into the water).

▶ *From the square, continue up Via Fieschi to the...*

End-of-Town Viewpoint

The Santa Maria Belvedere, named for a church that once stood here, marks the scenic end of Corniglia. This is a super picnic spot. From here, look high to the west (right), where the village and sanctuary of San Bernardino straddle a ridge (accessible by shuttle bus or a long uphill hike from Vernazza). Way down below are the local swimming hole and huge sunning rocks.

EXPERIENCES IN CORNIGLIA

Hikes from Corniglia

From Corniglia you can hike on the coastal trail to **Vernazza.** Also consider the challenging but rewarding "high road" to **Manarola via Volastra.** For details, see "Hiking the Cinque Terre" on page 22.

SLEEPING IN CORNIGLIA

Because Corniglia has no harbor, its mostly humble accommodations are almost never full.

$$ Villa Cecio (pronounced "chay-choh") sits atop the old-time Ristorante Cecio (with great views). They offer eight freshly decorated, well-priced, sizeable rooms on the quiet outskirts of town. Most rooms have postcard views, and three have terraces—worth requesting when you book. All rooms share a big rooftop view terrace (breakfast extra, 4 rooms have air-con, on main road toward Vernazza at Via Serra 58— keep going 200 yards beyond Ciappà square and you'll find it on the right, +39 0187 812 043, mobile +39 351 566 3661, www.cecio5terre.com, cecio5terre@gmail.com, Cristina and Valentina). They also rent eight more rooms in an annex on the square where the bus stops.

$$ Il Carugio has six modern, fresh, sunny rooms, and a communal rooftop terrace with a commanding view of the coast. Five of the rooms have a kitchen (2-night minimum, family rooms, air-con, no breakfast, free parking, free self-serve laundry, +39 0187 812 293, mobile +39 339 228 3803 or +39 338 112 6504, www.ilcarugiodicorniglia.

com, info@ilcarugiodicorniglia.com, Lidia and Giulia). They also have four more rooms, with breakfast included, in another building.

$ Cristiana Ricci rents three small, clean, and peaceful rooms—one with a terrace and sweeping view—just inland from the bus stop (family rooms, check in and breakfast at Pan e Vin bar at Via Fieschi 123, +39 338 937 6547, www.corniglia-room.com, cri_affittacamere@virgilio.it). She also rents three big, modern apartments.

¢ Corniglia Hostel, the town's former schoolhouse, rents 24 beds in a yellow municipal building up some steps from the square where the bus stops (find the entrance at the back of the building). Despite its institutional atmosphere, the hostel's prices, central location, and bright, clean rooms ensure its popularity. Its hotelesque double rooms are open to anyone (breakfast extra, office open 15:00-20:00, free lockers when office closed, air-con, self-serve laundry, Via alla Stazione 3, +39 0187 812 559, www.ostellocorniglia.com, ostellocorniglia@gmail.com, Alessandro).

EATING IN CORNIGLIA

A typical array of pizzerias, *focaccerie,* and alimentari (grocery stores) line the narrow main drag. I've highlighted a few places for a quick bite on my self-guided walk, earlier.

For a full, sit-down meal, consider one of these restaurants.

$$$ Ristorante il Buongustaio is a good bet for dinner on the square. Daniela and the Guelfi family pride themselves in serving *cucina casalinga* (home cooking) and good seafood pasta and risotto (nice tables on the main square as well as in a big indoor dining room, daily 12:00-21:15, Via Fieschi 164, +39 0187 821 424).

$$ Osteria Mananan—between the Ciappà bus stop and the main square at Via Fieschi 117—has earned a good reputation with tasty dishes and a small, stony, elegant interior (Wed-Mon 12:30-14:30 & 19:00-22:30, closed Tue, no outdoor seating, +39 0187 821 166, Agostino).

$$ Enoteca il Pirùn, on Via Fieschi, has a small restaurant above the wine bar, where Mario serves typical local dishes (Fri-Wed 12:00-16:00 & 19:00-23:30, closed Thu, +39 0187 812 315).

$$ La Posada Ristorante serves seafood in a tree-shaded garden overlooking the sea and in a modern interior. It's at the top of the stairs that lead down to the station, just outside the old center (daily 12:00-16:00 & 19:00-23:00, +39 333 454 2113).

Manarola

Mellow Manarola fills a ravine, bookended by its wild little harbor to the west and a diminutive hilltop church square inland to the east. Manarola is exceptional for being unexceptional: While Vernazza is prettier, Monterosso glitzier, Riomaggiore bigger, and Corniglia more rustic, Manarola hits a fine balance, giving it the "just right" combination of Cinque Terre qualities. Perhaps that's why it's a favorite among savvy Europeans seeking a relatively untrampled home base.

Manarola, whose hillsides are blanketed with vineyards, also provides the easiest access to the Cinque Terre's remarkable dry-stone terraces. The trail ringing the town's cemetery, on the peninsula north of the main harbor, affords some of the most strikingly beautiful town views anywhere in the region.

ORIENTATION TO MANAROLA

The touristy zone squeezed between the cement-encased train tracks and the harbor can be stressfully congested, but head just a few steps uphill and you can breathe again. Follow my gentle self-guided stroll from the harbor up through town, then through vineyards, to this stunning Mediterranean viewpoint.

Tourist Information

The TI/national park information office is in the train station (daily 8:30-19:30, shorter hours off-season).

Arrival in Manarola

By Train: From the station, to reach the town, you'll walk through a 200-yard-long tunnel that's lined with interesting photos. (During WWII air raids, these tunnels provided refuge and a safe place for rattled villagers to sleep.) To reach the busy harbor—with touristy restaurants, a boat dock, and the start of my self-guided walk—head left (downhill) when you come out of the tunnel.

The ATC **shuttle bus** runs from near the old waterwheel (halfway up Manarola's main street), stopping first at the parking lots above town, and then going all the way up to Volastra (about 2/hour except for afternoon breaks).

By Car: If you're overnighting here, ask your hotelier for parking advice. Park your car in one of the two pay lots just before town, then walk down the road to the church; from there it's an easy downhill walk to the main piazza, train-station tunnel, and harbor (the start of my self-guided walk), or you can wait for the shuttle bus.

Manarola has picturesque perches...

...and an artsy square.

MANAROLA WALK

From the harbor, this 45-minute self-guided walk shows you the town and surrounding vineyards and ends at a fantastic viewpoint.

▶ *Start down at the waterfront. Belly up to the wooden banister overlooking the rocky harbor, between the two restaurants.*

Harbor

Manarola is tiny and picturesque, a tumble of buildings bunny-hopping down its ravine to the fun-loving waterfront. The **breakwater,** which attempts to make this jagged harbor a bit less dangerous, was built (with reject marble from Carrara) just over a decade ago. Notice how the I-beam crane launches boats (which must be pulled ashore when bad weather is expected, to avoid being smashed or swept away).

Facing the water, look up to the right, at the hillside Punta Bonfiglio **cemetery** and park. The trail running around the base of the point—where this walk ends—offers magnificent views back on this part of town.

The town's **swimming hole** is just below you. Manarola has no sand but offers the best deep-water swimming in the area. The first "beach" has a shower, a ladder, and wonderful rocks. The second has tougher access and no shower but feels more remote and pristine (follow the paved path toward Corniglia, just around the point).

▶ *Go inland up the town's main drag. You'll climb a concrete ramp to Manarola's "new" square, which covers the train tracks, and is called...*

Piazza Capellini

Built in 2004, this square is an all-around great idea, giving the town a safe, fun zone for kids. Locals living near the tracks also enjoy a little less train noise. The mosaic in the middle of the square depicts the varieties of local fish in colorful enamel.

▶ *Go down the stairs at the upper end of the square. On your right, notice the tunnel that leads to Manarola's train station (and the closed Via dell'Amore trailhead). Head up...*

Via Discovolo

Manarola's main street twists up through town, lined by modest shops and filled with pooped hikers. About 100 yards up, just before

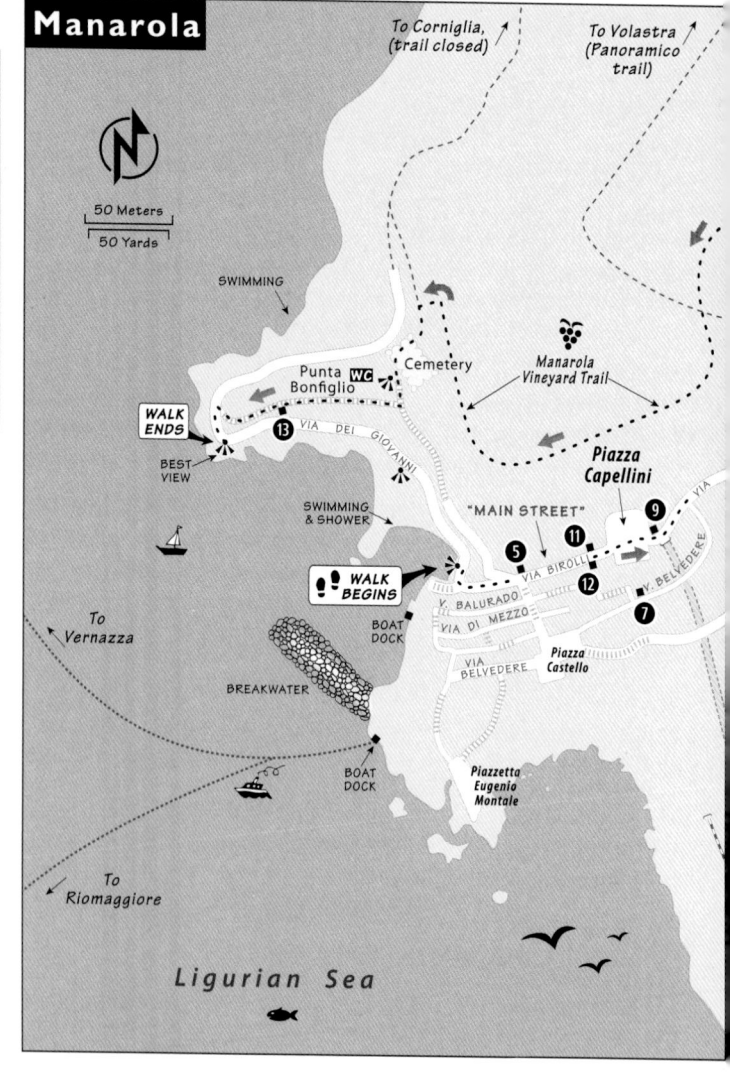

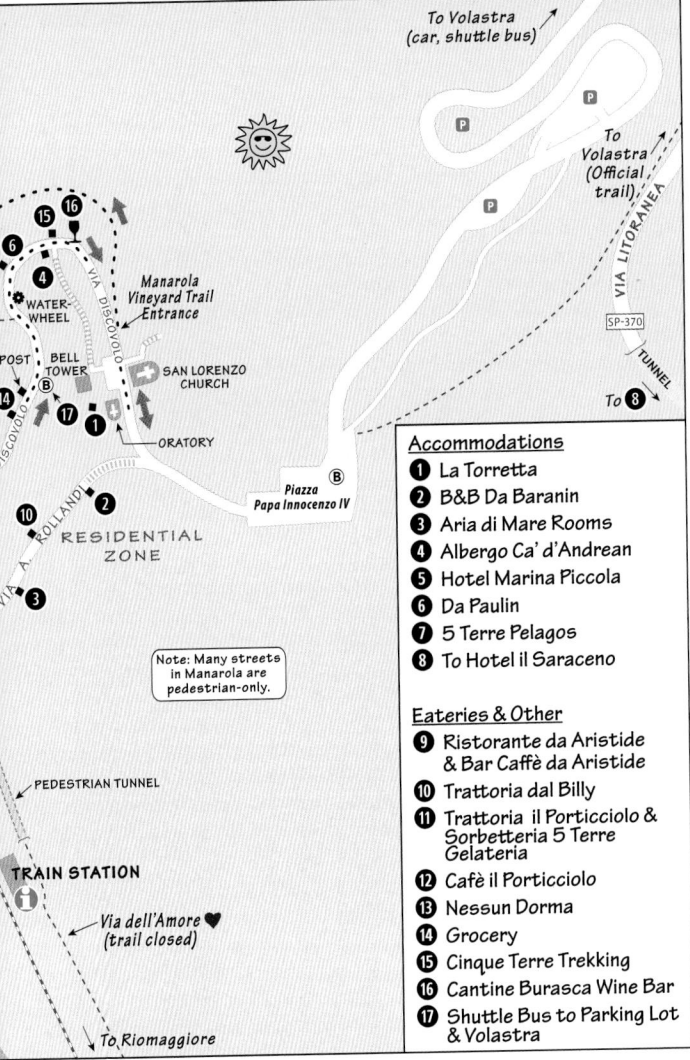

To Volastra
(car, shuttle bus)

To Volastra
(Official trail)

VIA LITORANEA

SP-370

TUNNEL

To ⑧

Manarola
Vineyard Trail
Entrance

VIA DISCOVOLO

WATER-
WHEEL

⑮ ⑯

⑥

④

POST

BELL
TOWER

Ⓑ

⑭

⑰

①

SAN LORENZO
CHURCH

ORATORY

DISCOVOLO

⑩

VIA A. ROLLANDI

②

③

RESIDENTIAL
ZONE

Piazza
Papa Innocenzo IV

Ⓑ

Note: Many streets
in Manarola are
pedestrian-only.

PEDESTRIAN TUNNEL

TRAIN STATION

Via dell'Amore ♥
(trail closed)

To Riomaggiore

Accommodations

① La Torretta
② B&B Da Baranin
③ Aria di Mare Rooms
④ Albergo Ca' d'Andrean
⑤ Hotel Marina Piccola
⑥ Da Paulin
⑦ 5 Terre Pelagos
⑧ To Hotel il Saraceno

Eateries & Other

⑨ Ristorante da Aristide
   & Bar Caffè da Aristide
⑩ Trattoria dal Billy
⑪ Trattoria il Porticciolo &
   Sorbetteria 5 Terre
   Gelateria
⑫ Cafè il Porticciolo
⑬ Nessun Dorma
⑭ Grocery
⑮ Cinque Terre Trekking
⑯ Cantine Burasca Wine Bar
⑰ Shuttle Bus to Parking Lot
   & Volastra

the road bends sharply right, watch (on the right) for a **waterwheel.** One possible origin of the town's name is that it's local dialect for "big wheel." A waterwheel like this once powered local industry. As you continue up (all the way to the church), you'll still hear the rushing waters of Manarola's stream. Like those in Riomaggiore, Monterosso, and Vernazza, Manarola's rivulet was covered over after World War II. Before that time, romantic bridges arched over its ravine. You can peek below the concrete street in several places to see the stream surging below your feet.

Across the street from the waterwheel and a bit farther up, notice the **Cinque Terre Trekking** shop on your left, which outfits hikers with both information and gear (for details, see "Hikes from Manarola," later).

Around the corner is the **Cantine Burasca** wine bar with fine outdoor-only seating (closed in bad weather, Via Discovolo 86, +39 339 807 1261).

▸ *Keep climbing until you come to the square at the...*

Top of Manarola

The square is faced by a church, an oratory—now a religious and community meeting place—and a bell tower (with a WWI memorial etched in it), which served as a watchtower when pirates raided the town (the cupola was added once the attacks ceased). To the right of the oratory, a stepped lane leads to the town's sizable, less-touristy residential zone.

Check out the **church.** The Parish Church of St. Lawrence (San Lorenzo) dates from "MCCCXXXVIII" (1338). Step inside to see two altarpiece paintings from the unnamed Master of the Cinque Terre, the only painter of any note from this region (left wall and above main altar). While the style is Gothic, the work dates from the time of Michelangelo, long after Florence had entered the Renaissance. Note the humble painted stone ceiling, which replaced the wooden original in the 1800s. It features Lawrence, patron saint of the Cinque Terre, with his grill, the symbol of his martyrdom (he was roasted on it).

▸ *With the bell tower on your left, head about 20 yards back down the main street below the church and find a wooden railing on the right, just before the Cantine Burasca wine bar, signposted as* trail #502C. *It*

Enjoy the views along Manarola's vineyard walk.

marks the start of a delightful stroll around the high side of town and back to the seafront. This is the beginning of the...

Manarola Vineyard Trail

Don't miss this fun, short walk. Simply follow the wooden railing, enjoying lemon groves and great views. Along the path, which is largely flat, you'll get a close-up look at the region's famous dry-stone walls and finely crafted vineyards (with dried-heather thatches to protect the grapes from southwest winds). Smell the rosemary. Study the structure of the town, and pick out the scant remains of an old fort. Notice the S-shape of the main road—once a riverbed—that flows through town. The town's roofs are traditionally made of locally quarried slate and held down by rocks during windstorms.

Halfway along the lip of the ravine, a path marked *Panoramico Volastra (Corniglia)* leads steeply up into the vineyards (a challenging route that leads to the tiny hamlet of Volastra and then to Corniglia—described on page 28).

Stay on the level path, passing a variety of simple wooden religious scenes, the work of local resident Mario Andreoli. Before his father died, Mario promised him he'd replace the old cross on the family's vineyard. Mario has been adding figures ever since. On religious holidays, everything's lit up: the Nativity, the Last Supper, the Crucifixion, the Resurrection, and more. Some of the scenes are left up year-round. (You can see more of his figures across the ravine, gathered together in a little open patch between buildings.) High above, notice ancient terraces that line the terrain like a topographic map.

▶ *Continue on the trail as it winds down to the cemetery (sometimes closed, but at least stop by the gate for a peek inside).*

Cemetery

Ever since Napoleon—who was king of Italy in the early 1800s—decreed that cemeteries were health risks, Cinque Terre's burial spots have been located outside the towns. The result: The dearly departed generally get first-class sea views. Each cemetery—with evocative photos and finely carved Carrara marble memorial reliefs—is worth a look. Manarola's is a little lower down and easier to walk to than the others.

In cemeteries like these, the wealthy get their own piece of land (a **grave**), regular people get the equivalent of a condo (with their remains parked in a niche called a **loculus**), and the poor and forgotten end up tossed in a communal **ossuary.** Because of the tight space, spots are rented and a person's remains are allowed to stay only as long as their loved ones pay the rent. (No rent means you end up in the ossuary.) Traditionally, locals make weekly visits to loved ones here, often bringing flowers. The rolling stepladder makes access to top-floor loculi easy.

▶ *From the cemetery follow the steep and narrow stairs (through the green gate immediately below the cemetery) and walk out onto the bluff.*

Manarola's cemetery has a sea view...

...as do its scenic and winding trails.

Punta Bonfiglio

This point offers some of the most commanding **views** of the entire region. To find the best vantage point, walk out toward the water through a park (playground, drinking water, WC, and picnic benches). An inviting and recommended bar, **Nessun Dorma,** fills a long narrow terrace with people enjoying the vista.

Your Manarola finale is the bench at the tip of the point. (It's often congested with travelers taking photos from this point for their Instagram bucket lists.) Pause and take in the view.

▶ *From here steps go down and the path winds scenically back to the harbor, where we started.*

EXPERIENCES IN MANAROLA

Hikes from Manarola

The coastal trail from Manarola—leading to **Corniglia** in one direction and to **Riomaggiore** in the other (the famous Via dell'Amore)—has been closed for years due to landslides. But you can still enjoy hiking from here. One of my favorite easy hikes is the **vineyards trail** outlined just above in my "Manarola Walk."

For a longer hike, consider taking the **high route to Corniglia via Volastra** (much easier if you ride the shuttle bus up to Volastra). For details, see "Hiking the Cinque Terre" on page 22.

Hiking Gear and Tips: A wonderful resource for hikers, **Cinque Terre Trekking is** near the top of the main street (halfway up to the church). Christine (from Minnesota) and Nicola are generous with hiking advice, and fill their shop with all the gear you may need: boots, clothes, walking sticks, maps, and more. If you're serious about hiking, stop in here to confirm your plans and to gear up (daily 11:00-13:00 & 14:00-19:00, shorter hours off-season, Via Discovolo 108, +39 0187 920 834, www.cinqueterretrekking.com, info@cinqueterretrekking.com).

Pesto Making

Entrepreneurial Simone at the Nessun Dorma cantina (perched next to the cemetery at the most scenic edge of Manarola) leads a pesto-making workshop for up to 30 people at 10:30, followed by lunch at noon. The setting is unforgettable, making pesto in the place of its origin is exciting, and you get to eat what you make plus a *tagliere* plate of cold cuts (€60/person, includes wine, no class on Tue, reserve ahead at www.nessundormacinqueterre.com or call +39 340 888 4133, canceled in bad weather).

Tours

Arbaspàa arranges vineyard wine tastings, cooking classes (6-person minimum), fishing trips, paragliding, rock climbing, and more (see website for options and book in advance, www.arbaspaa.com; or visit office at Via Discovolo 204, daily 9:00-19:00, +39 0187 760 083).

Boat Rides

To get to the dock and the boats that connect Manarola with the other Cinque Terre towns, find the steps to the left of the harbor view—they lead down to the ticket kiosk. Continue around the left side of the cliff (as you're facing the water) to catch the boats.

SLEEPING IN MANAROLA

Manarola has some of the most appealing, well-run accommodations in the region (rivaling Monterosso's). Like the others, it also has plenty of private rooms (Airbnb has consumed the market). If you need breakfast, the recommended Bar Caffè da Aristide is your best choice. Otherwise grab a coffee and croissant along the main drag.

In the Residential Zone Above the Church

This area is a 10-minute steeply uphill hike from the train station—just huff up the main drag to the church. All are within a five-minute walk from there.

$$$$ La Torretta offers 16 trendy, upscale rooms (most with private deck) that cater to an elite clientele. Probably the most elegant retreat in the region, this peaceful refuge has all the comforts for those happy to pay, including a communal hot tub with a view. Guests enjoy a complimentary snack and glass of prosecco on arrival, an ample breakfast buffet, and stocked minibars. Each chic room is distinct (top-end family suite, book several months in advance, closed Dec-March; on Piazza della Chiesa beside the bell tower at Vico Volto 20, +39 0187 920 327, www.torrettas.com, torretta@cdh.it, Gabriele).

$$$ B&B Da Baranin, with eight good rooms and one apartment, is a bit too pricey but has sleek modern style and a nice breakfast terrace (family rooms, air-con, Via Aldo Rollandi 29, +39 0187 920 595, www.baranin.com, info@baranin.com).

$$ Aria di Mare Rooms rents four sunny, tidy, well-equipped rooms and two apartments a few steps beyond Trattoria dal Billy at the very top of town. While it's a steep hike up (high above the tourists), this is an excellent value. Three rooms and the two apartments have spacious terraces, and all can enjoy the knockout views from lounge chairs in the front yard (RS% with 4-night stay, no breakfast but tea/coffee service in room, air-con, up the stairs at Via Aldo Rollandi 149, +39 349 058 4155, www.ariadimare.info, info@ariadimare.info, Maurizio; ask at Billy's if no one's home).

On or near the Main Street

These options line up along (or near) the main street, between the harbor and the church. While in a less atmospheric area than those near the church, they're closer to the station, and therefore a bit handier for those packing heavy.

$$$ Albergo Ca' d'Andrean is quiet, comfortable, and chic. It has 10 big, sunny, tranquil rooms, with lots of tile. Public spaces artfully display family artifacts, and the cool garden oasis comes complete with lemon trees. If you don't mind stairs, consider one of their pricier top-floor rooms, with great terrace views (breakfast extra, air-con, up the hill at Via Discovolo 101, +39 0187 920 040, www.cadandrean.it, info@cadandrean.it, Simone, Ariana, and Nicola).

$$$ Hotel Marina Piccola offers 12 simple, stylish rooms near the bustle of the square on the water (some with sea views). Though low on character, it's well run and handy to the harbor area (breakfast extra, air-con, Via Birolli 120, +39 0187 920 770, www.hotelmarinapiccola.com, info@hotelmarinapiccola.com, Jessica and Micaela).

$$ Da Paulin, run by charming Donatella (who makes a mean *limoncello*) and Eraldo (the town's retired policeman), has three surprisingly modern, fresh, well-equipped, hotelesque rooms with a large and inviting common living room. They also rent three apartments (with fans). This fine value is at the bend in the main street, a five-minute hike above the train tracks (breakfast extra, air-con, Via Discovolo 126, +39 334 389 4764, www.dapaulin.it, prenotazioni@dapaulin.it).

$$ 5 Terre Pelagos has eight pastel, shabby-chic rooms in two buildings. Four are at Via Belvedere 58, an awkward building down a side lane. Built into the side of the mountain, the common room has a caveman ambience, but some rooms come with view terraces. The other rooms are more steeply uphill near the church, at Via dei Mulini 26—confirm which building you are in when you book (air-con, +39 335 122 6490, www.5terrepelagos.com, info@5terrepelagos.com, Edoardo).

High Above Manarola, in Volastra

$$ Hotel il Saraceno, with seven spacious, utilitarian rooms, is a deal for drivers. Located above Manarola in the tiny town of Volastra (chock-full of vacationing Germans and Italians in summer), it's serene, clean, and right by the shuttle bus to Manarola (includes breakfast, free parking, air-con, +39 0187 760 081, www.thesaraceno.com, hotel@thesaraceno.com, friendly Antonella).

EATING IN MANAROLA

Touristy restaurants are concentrated between Piazza Capellini and the harbor. For finer dining, consider one of the following choices.

$$ Ristorante da Aristide, right on Piazza Capellini, is run by three generations of hardworking women and offers a trendy atmosphere and a pleasant outdoor setting, with a view of budding soccer stars rather than harborfront glitz. Consider the €45 three-course meal with wine (Fri-Wed 12:00-15:00 & 19:00-22:00, closed Thu, Via Discovolo 290—you run right into it from the train tunnel, +39 0187 920 000).

$$ Bar Caffè da Aristide, next door along the street, is a busy and modern little place with reasonable prices. They have indoor and streetside seating, a lighter menu of pasta and salads (see daily specials on blackboard), and breakfast (Fri-Wed 8:00-11:30 & 12:00-18:00, closed Thu, same address and phone number; charming Elena, Mamma Monica, and Nonna Grazia).

$$$ Trattoria dal Billy, the most memorable restaurant in town, is in the residential zone high above the touristy action. It's worth the climb for Edoardo and chef Enrico's homemade black pasta with seafood and squid ink, green pasta with artichokes, and homemade desserts. Their antipasto misto di mare comes with a dazzling array of

seafood treats—each one perfectly executed. Billy's outdoor terraces offer commanding views over Manarola, while across the street an elegant, glassy dining room is carved into the rock. Either setting is perfect for a romantic candlelight meal. Reservations are a must (Fri-Wed 12:00-15:00 & 18:00-22:00, closed Thu, Via Aldo Rollandi 122, +39 0187 920 628, www.trattoriabilly.com).

$$ Trattoria il Porticciolo is run by the hard-working Scorza family (Thu-Tue 12:00-15:00 & 19:00-21:30, closed Wed, Via Birolli 92, +39 0187 920 083). They also run the cheap, fast, and contemporary **cafè** across the way.

Drinks and Light Meals with a View

$$ Nessun Dorma is dramatically perched under the cemetery and above the harbor, facing the classic view of Manarola. Simone and his staff serve no pizza or pasta, but keep the masses happy with bruschetta, cold cuts, salads, and tempting cocktails. This place has become inundated with Instagram influencers and scenesters, so there can be long lines waiting for a table (no reservations). It's named for a Puccini aria made famous by Pavarotti, whose face graces the menu (Wed-Mon 12:00-21:00, closed Tue, Localita Punta Bonfiglio, +39 340 888 4133, www.nessundormacinqueterre.com). Simone runs a morning pesto-making class that culminates in a scenic lunch just before opening time—perhaps the most peaceful (and educational) way to enjoy this beautiful spot (described earlier, under "Experiences in Manarola").

Quick Bites and Takeout

Via Discovolo, the main street climbing up through town from Piazza Capellini to the church, has several shops selling focaccia, pizza by the slice, and fried goodies that are perfect for a quick lunch. Buy picnic supplies at the **Co-op grocery** at #224 (daily 7:30-13:00 & 17:00-20:00). **Bar Caffè da Aristide** is the busiest for breakfast. And the most enticing *gelateria* in town is **Sorbetteria 5 Terre Gelateria** (below the piazza, toward the harbor).

Riomaggiore

The second-largest of the five towns, Riomaggiore is more real and laid-back than its neighbors. The main drag, while traffic-free, feels more urban than village. Despite Riomaggiore's workaday soul, the views back on its harbor from the breakwater—especially at sunset—are some of the region's prettiest. Surrounding the harbor is a fascinating tangle of pastel homes leaning on each other like drunken sailors.

ORIENTATION TO RIOMAGGIORE

Tourist Information

The **national park office** and InfoPoint is in the striped building adjacent to the station (daily 8:30-19:30, shorter hours off-season).

Arrival in Riomaggiore

By Train: Riomaggiore's train station is in the next ravine over from the village, separated from the town center by a bluff. To get to the center quickly, take the pedestrian tunnel that parallels the rail tunnel. You'll exit at the bottom of Via Colombo; most recommended accommodations are a short hike up this steep main drag. If you're staying near the top of town, you can catch the sporadic shuttle bus at the bottom of Via Colombo and ride it partway up.

If you're not in a hurry or carrying luggage, take the scenic route around the bluff into town, which gives you a better feel for life here—see my "Riomaggiore Walk," later.

By Car: Day-trippers park at the two-story pay-and-display lot above town (€5/hour, €35/day). If you're staying overnight, your hotel may have parking.

Helpful Hints

Baggage Storage: You can check your bag at the casually run ***deposito bagagli*** office—it's behind the café/bar that's straight ahead as you exit the station (daily 9:00-12:30 & 14:00-19:00—confirm times, closed in winter).

Services: There are three public pay WCs in town: at the station and at the top and bottom of Via Colombo.

Workaday Riomaggiore feels lived in.

Here, every day is laundry day.

Laundry: A self-service launderette is on the main street (daily in summer 8:00-23:00, shorter hours off-season, Via Colombo 107).

RIOMAGGIORE WALK

Here's an easy self-guided walk that loops up and over, taking the long and scenic way from the station into town. You'll enjoy some fine views and get to know the town before strolling down the main street to the harbor.

▶ *Start at the train station. (If you arrive by boat, cross beneath the tracks and take a left, then hike through the tunnel along the tracks to reach the station.)*

Climb to the Top of Town

With your back to the sea and station, look left and notice the stairs climbing up just past the station building. These lead to the easy (but closed) trail to Manarola, the **Via dell'Amore.**

Now hike up Via Telemaco Signorini (next to Bar Stazione). Listen to the paved-over creek under your feet. Where the road hairpins right, see the waterfall (and turtles in the cage). Farther along is a close-up look at dry-stone rockery work. You'll cross over the train tracks, passing the top of a concrete elevator tower. Just beyond the elevator, you'll arrive at a fine viewpoint, with spectacular sea views and a few benches.

▶ *When you're ready to move on, hook left around the bluff; rounding the bend, ignore the steps marked marina seacoast (which lead to the harbor). Look on your left for the stairway marked* Salita Castello, *across from house #179. If you're up for a steep side trip, climb a few flights of stairs to the...*

Riomaggiore Castle

The castle, a hulk at the top of the hill, is usually shut up tight, but it's sometimes used for cultural events. You'll find great sea views from benches in front, and the tiny church of San Rocco (built for plague victims, and therefore outside of the town walls).

▶ *Descend the way you came up.*

Riomaggiore

To Manarola
(trail closed)

♥ Via dell'Amore ♥
(trail closed)

Cliffs

TRAIN STATION

GATE

NATIONAL PARK SHOP

Ligurian Sea

WATERFALL

VIA TELEMACO SIGNORINI

⓭

⓲

WALK BEGINS

ELEVATOR

SAN ROCCO   V. PECUNI

CASTLE

CITY HALL

PEDESTRIAN TUNNEL

VIA TELEMACO SIGNORINI

VIA SANT'ANTONIO

VIA PUNTA

Piazza Vignaioli

⓬

❼

WC
(UNDER TUNNEL)

Cliffs

❻

❶

⓴

⓰

Harbor

BOAT DOCK

BREAKWATER

VIA GIACOMO

BOAT TICKETS

Accommodations

❶ Alla Marina; Enoteca & Ristorante Dau Cila
❷ Casato Bapò
❸ Il BoMa
❹ La Dolce Vita
❺ Edi's

Eateries & Other

❻ Rio Bistrot
❼ Trattoria la Grotta
❽ Bar Centrale & Gelateria
❾ Primo Piatto & Vertical Lounge Bar
❿ Il Pescato Cucinato
⓫ Tutti Fritti
⓬ Alimentari Franca
⓭ Bar Stazione
⓮ Bar & Vini A Piè de Mà
⓯ La Zorza Café & Bar O'Netto
⓰ La Conchiglia Café/Bar

⓱ Grocery (2)
⓲ Bag Storage
⓳ Launderette
⓴ Diving Center 5 Terre

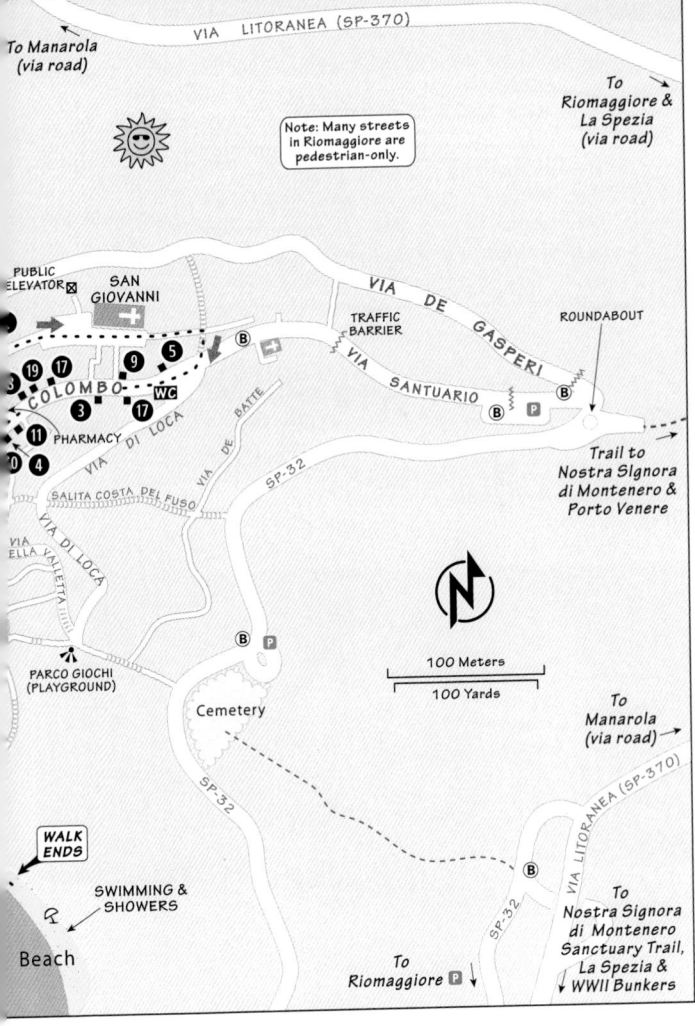

To Manarola
(via road)

VIA LITORANEA (SP-370)

To
Riomaggiore &
La Spezia
(via road)

Note: Many streets
in Riomaggiore are
pedestrian-only.

PUBLIC
ELEVATOR

SAN
GIOVANNI

VIA DE GASPERI

ROUNDABOUT

TRAFFIC
BARRIER

VIA SANTUARIO

COLOMBO

WC

PHARMACY

VIA DI LOCA

VIA DE BATTE

SP-32

Trail to
Nostra Signora
di Montenero &
Porto Venere

SALITA COSTA DEL FUSO

VIA
ELLA VALETTA

VIA DI LOCA

PARCO GIOCHI
(PLAYGROUND)

Cemetery

100 Meters

100 Yards

To
Manarola
(via road)

SP-32

WALK
ENDS

SWIMMING &
SHOWERS

Beach

To
Riomaggiore

VIA LITORANEA (SP-370)

SP-32

To
Nostra Signora
di Montenero
Sanctuary Trail,
La Spezia &
WWII Bunkers

Town Views and Church of San Giovanni Battista (St. John the Baptist)

Continuing along the smooth and level lane, you'll go by the **City Hall** (with flags) and several decaying **murals** by Silvio Benedetto. These glorify the region's nameless workers—grape pickers, fishermen, and everyone who built the nearly 300 million cubic feet of mortarless, dry-stone walls that run throughout the Cinque Terre. These walls give the region its characteristic terracing for vineyards and olive groves. Unfortunately, the murals are not aging well.

You'll next reach a piazza and the gray stone San Giovanni church. Pause here at the big **terrace** to enjoy the views over town, perhaps with lots of local kids (schools are close by). The town is named after its large (*maggiore*) river (*rio*), now covered by the main street, as in the other Cinque Terre towns. The river carved the canyon now filled by the town's pastel highrises. The romantic arched bridges that once connected the two sides have been replaced by a practical modern road. Other than that, the town is beautifully preserved.

The **church,** while rebuilt in 1870, was first established in 1340. It's dedicated to St. John the Baptist, the patron saint of Genoa, the maritime republic that once dominated the region.

A Silvio Benedetto mural celebrates working-class Ligurians.

▶ *Continue straight past the church and along the narrow lane leading down to the town's main street, and hang a right on...*

Via Colombo

This street has the town's shops and services. Heading downhill, the big covered terrace on the right belongs to the recommended **Bar Centrale,** a popular hangout for international visitors day or night.

As you round the bend to the left, notice the old-timey pharmacy just above (on the right, with a good bakery underneath). On your left, at #199, peek into the **Il Pescato Cucinato** shop, where Laura fries up her husband, Edoardo's, fresh catch; grab a paper cone of deep-fried seafood as a snack. Where the road bends sharply right, notice the bench on your left (just before La Zorza Café)—the hangout for the town's old-timers, who keep a running commentary on the steady flow of people. Straight ahead, you can already see where this street will dead-end. The last shop on the left, **Alimentari Franca** (at #251), is a well-stocked grocery where you can gather the makings for a perfect picnic out on the harbor.

Where Via Colombo dead-ends, look right to see the tunnel leading back to the station. Look left to see two sets of stairs. Climb the "up" stairs to a parklike **square** (Piazza Vignaioli) built over the train tracks, which provides the children of the town a bit of level land on which to kick their soccer balls and to learn to ride a bike. The murals above, marking the town's middle school, celebrate the great-grandparents of these very children—the salt-of-the-earth locals who earned a humble living before the age of tourism. Riomaggiorians are proud that they are the only Cinque Terre town with their own middle school (*scuola media*)—in the other towns, kids start commuting to school much earlier.

▶ *Now take the "down" stairs to the...*

Harbor

In this most picturesque corner of Riomaggiore, a tight cluster of buildings huddles nervously around a tiny square and harbor. Because Riomaggiore lacks the naturally protected harbor of Vernazza, when bad weather is expected, fishermen pull their boats up to the safety of the little square. This is quite an operation, so it's a team effort—the signal goes out, and anyone with a boat of their own helps move the whole fleet. Sometimes the fishermen are busy beaching their boats even on a bright, sunny day—an indication that they know something you don't.

Riomaggiore's beach scene is busy by day...   ...and romantic by night.

A couple of recommended restaurants—with high prices and memorable seating—look down over the action. Head past them and up the walkway along the left side of the harbor, and enjoy the **views** back at the town's colorful pastel buildings, with the craggy coastline of the Cinque Terre just beyond. The best views are from up top, at the edge of the bluff. Below you, the breakwater (made of reject marble blocks from the famous nearby quarries of Carrara) curves out to sea, providing a bit of protection for the harbor. These rocks are popular with sunbathers by day and romantics and photographers at sunset.

For a peek at Riomaggiore's beach, continue around the bluff on this trail toward Punta di Montenero, the cape that defines the southern end of the Cinque Terre. As you walk, you'll pass the rugged boat landing and eventually run into Riomaggiore's uncomfortably rocky but still inviting beach (*spiaggia*). Ponder how Europeans manage to look relaxed when lounging on football-sized "pebbles."

EXPERIENCES IN RIOMAGGIORE

Hikes from Riomaggiore

For an **easy walk** along the lip of the one-time river ravine, take **Via di Loca,** which veers off Via Colombo at the top of town (directly across from the stairs at the upper end of Via Colombo). This leads in just a few minutes to the town playground (*parco giochi*), benches, neighborhood pea patches, and pleasant views over town (especially at sunset). There's also a steep staircase from here up to the town cemetery; from there, an even steeper trail runs all the way up to the town's 14th-century **Nostra Signora di Montenero sanctuary,** high above the town.

For an easier climb to the sanctuary, opt for the **scenic one-hour trail** that rises from the top of town. Take the main road inland until you see signs at the roundabout at the end of Via Santuario; or ride the shuttle bus 12 minutes from the town center to the sanctuary trail, then walk uphill another 20 minutes (great picnic spot up top).

Beach

Riomaggiore's rugged and tiny "beach" is rocky, but it's clean and peaceful. It's just around the bluff from the harbor, past the boat landing—to find it, see the end of my self-guided walk, earlier. There's a shower here in the summer, and another closer to town by the boat landing—where many enjoy sunning on and jumping from the rocks.

Kayaks and Water Sports

Diving Center 5 Terre rents kayaks as well as snorkeling and scuba equipment; they also lead guided dives of the protected marine waters nearby (open only in good weather, underground office in the passage leading to the harbor—down the stairs and under the tracks, Via San Giacomo, +39 0187 920 011, www.5terrediving.it).

NIGHTLIFE IN RIOMAGGIORE

With a youthful spirit and lively evening bustle, Riomaggiore has an enjoyable night scene. Stroll the main drag, scope out these listings (serving €6-8 cocktails), and find the one that appeals. Several of these places have full menus if you want to eat.

Bar Centrale, run by sociable Ivo, Alberto, and the gang, offers "nightlife" any time of day—it's a magnet for tourists. Ivo, who lived in the Bay Area, fills his bar with San Franciscan rock and a fun-loving vibe; it feels a little like the village's living room (great mojitos, daily 7:30-late, Via Colombo 144).

Bar & Vini A Piè de Mà, above the train station at the now-closed Via dell'Amore trailhead, has piles of charm and frequent music, and stays open until 23:00 from June through September.

More Bars and Cafés: Near the bottom of Via Colombo, facing each other, are the noisy **La Zorza Café** (appealing to international tourists with thumping music and freestyle bartenders) and the classier **Bar O'Netto** (geared more for young locals, with a mellower vibe and nice outdoor seating). Higher up on Via Colombo (at #76), **Vertical Lounge Bar** has a lively and loose ambience, light food (a

Riomaggiore's breakwater is the perfect spot to watch the sun go down and the lights come up.

good aperitivo buffet at happy-hour time), and a fine people-watching perch near the top of the promenade zone. And at sunset, you can't beat **La Conchiglia**—the simple café/bar (closed Wed) on the bluff overlooking the harbor—a perfect location for watching the sun disappear into the Ligurian Sea and the lights of Monterosso twinkling on the horizon.

SLEEPING IN RIOMAGGIORE

Riomaggiore has few hotels worth your time; I recommend staying in one of the town's many private rooms for rent. Breakfast is normally on your own.

$$$ Alla Marina is Riomaggiore's best value, renting a half-dozen rooms and apartments—most with sea views—at the top of one of the tall, skinny buildings that rise up from the harbor. Friendly brothers Sandro and Andrea take pride in running a tight ship (RS%, breakfast extra, pay parking, office open 9:00-18:00, Via San Giacomo 61—ask about the easier back-door entrance, +39 328 013 4077, www.allamarina.com, info@allamarina.com). They also rent several other rooms in Riomaggiore and Manarola.

$$$ Casato Bapò has three airy, spacious rooms with unobstructed views at the top of town near the Church of San Giovanni. They're on the fourth floor, but accessible via the public elevator nearby (Via Pecunia 116, +39 340 705 6723, www.casatobapo.com, casatobapo@gmail.com, Sabrina).

$$ Il BoMa—named for the owners, American Maddy and her Italian husband, Bombetta—has three old-fashioned rooms along the main drag (one cheaper room with private bath down the hall, air-con, up 3 flights at Via Colombo 99, +39 0187 920 395, mobile +39 320 074 8826, www.ilboma5terre.com, info@ilboma5terre.com). They also rent two nearby apartments.

$$ La Dolce Vita offers six modern, good-value rooms on the main drag, plus two apartments elsewhere in town (some with air-con, open daily 9:30-19:30—if they're closed, they're full; Via Colombo 167, +39 331 903 6704, agonatal@libero.it, helpful Giacomo and Simone).

$$ Edi manages three rooms and an apartment. You pay extra for views (most rooms with air-con, reception at Via Colombo 12, +39 320 111 7074, www.appartamenticinqueterre.net, edi-vesigna@iol.it).

$ **Amy Inman** (an American expat who runs the Cinque Terre Insider blog) and her Italian husband, Francesco, offer an apartment and three private rooms (RS%, cash only, air-con, +39 329 572 0138— WhatsApp messages welcomed, CinqueTerreinsider.com, amy@cinqueterreinsider.com).

EATING IN RIOMAGGIORE

For more options, see "Nightlife in Riomaggiore," earlier.

On the Harbor

Harborfront dining comes with slightly higher prices, a dressy ambience, and glorious views.

$$$$ **Enoteca & Ristorante Dau Cila** (pronounced "dow CHEE-lah") is decked out like a black-and-white movie set in an old boat shed with extra tables outside on a rustic deck over dinghies. Try their €25 seafood antipasto plate and listen to the waves lapping at the harbor below (daily 12:30-15:00 & 19:30-22:30, Via San Giacomo 65, +39 0187 760 032, Luca).

$$$$ **Rio Bistrot,** small and intimate at the top of the harbor, jazzes up its Ligurian cuisine with international influences. You can order à la carte from the short but well-designed menu, or try their €40-60 tasting menus (daily 12:30-16:00 & 19:00-22:00, Via San Giacomo 46, +39 0187 920 616, Manuel).

On the Main Street, Via Colombo

$$$ **Trattoria la Grotta,** right in the town center (with no view), has a passion for anchovies and mussels. You'll enjoy reliably good food surrounded by historical photos and wonderful stonework in a dramatic, dressy, cave-like setting (reservations smart, Thu-Tue 12:00-14:30 & 18:00-22:30, closed Wed, Via Colombo 247, +39 0187 920 187, mobile +39 346 260 8709, www.lagrottariomaggiore.it).

$$ **Bar Centrale** is a casual, family-friendly place for hamburgers, salads, and pesto. They also have a *gelateria* on site (long hours daily, see listing earlier, under "Nightlife in Riomaggiore").

Light Meals: Various handy carryout eateries along the main drag offer good lunches or snacks. **$ Primo Piatto,** at the top of town, offers takeaway handmade pastas and sauces, cooked to order on the spot (Wed-Mon 10:30-19:30 or later, closed Tue, Via Colombo 72, Roberta). For deep-fried seafood in a paper cone, **$ Il Pescato Cucinato** is where Edoardo fishes and his wife, Laura, fries (chalkboard out front explains what's fresh, daily 11:30-20:30, near the bottom of Via Colombo at #199). A few doors away, **$ Tutti Fritti** serves only freshly fried nibbles, including fish (daily 10:00-21:00, Via Colombo 161, Andrea and Isabella).

Picnics: Groceries and delis lining Via Colombo sell food to-go for a picnic at the harbor or beach. **Co-op** grocery stores have the best prices (at #122 and #205, closed Sun). For a more appetizing selection and good service, head to **Alimentari Franca,** on the main street by the train-station tunnel (daily 8:00-20:00, shorter hours off-season, Via Colombo 251).

Breakfast: Most of my recommended accommodations don't serve breakfast—or simply leave a coffee kettle and basic continental breakfast fixings in your room. For eggs or a good croissant-and-espresso fix, drop by **Bar Centrale** (listed earlier), or **Bar Stazione,** at the train station.

Near the Train Station

$$ Bar & Vini A Piè de Mà, at the trailhead on the Manarola end of town, is good for a scenic light bite or quiet drink at night. The bar, with great outdoor seating, is self-service: Head into the bar to place your order, then bring it out to your preferred perch (Wed-Mon 11:00-21:00, June-Sept until 23:00, closed Tue and off-season).

Near the Cinque Terre

The Cinque Terre is tops, but there's much more to the Italian Riviera. To the north of the Cinque Terre is a trio of beach towns: Levanto, the northern gateway to the Cinque Terre; Sestri Levante, stunningly situated on a narrow peninsula flanked by two beaches; and Santa Margherita Ligure, a thriving city with an active waterfront and easy connections to yacht-happy Portofino. At the south end of the Cinque Terre is the pretty resort of Porto Venere and the region's workaday transit hub, La Spezia.

The best of these towns—the high-end yin to the Cinque Terre's ramshackle yang—can be user-friendly home bases for day trips along the Riviera coast. But they are also worth visiting in their own right.

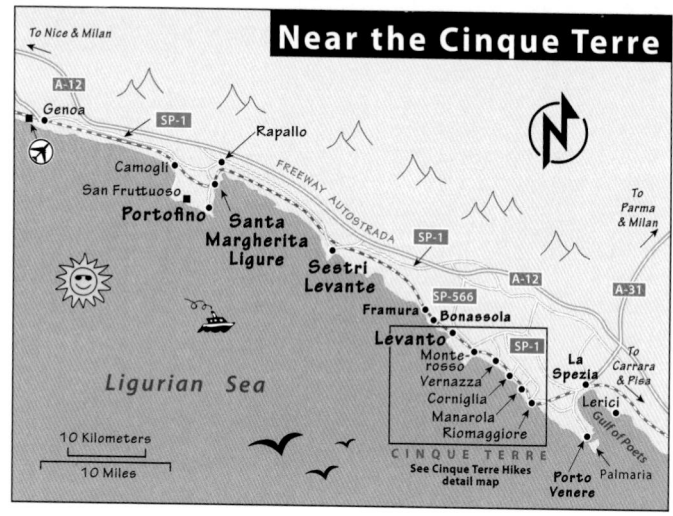

Near the Cinque Terre

Home Bases Near the Cinque Terre

Levanto, Sestri Levante, and Santa Margherita Ligure are practical home bases for those who want modern hotels with predictable resort amenities, and for drivers wanting to park at their hotel and side-trip to the Cinque Terre by train.

Levanto—just minutes north of Monterosso by train—is the handiest. Sestri Levante is a bit farther away with a little less train service. Santa Margherita Ligure is the most distant and often requires a transfer to the Cinque Terre, but compensates by being the most appealing—and it has easy access to posh Portofino. Porto Venere is better as a day trip, and La Spezia is more functional than appealing, although either can serve in a pinch.

Keep in mind that you'll be competing with other day-trippers for space on prime midday trains to and from the Cinque Terre. Turn this problem into an advantage: Enjoy your home-base town during the day, then head into the Cinque Terre in the late afternoon for untrampled charm, a romantic dinner, and a late train back.

North of the Cinque Terre

When most people imagine the "Italian Riviera," they're thinking of the shimmering resort towns north of the Cinque Terre. Stately Old World hotels loom over crowded pebble beaches with rentable umbrellas. Fastidiously landscaped parks and promenades are jammed with more Italian visitors than American tourists. These towns are perfect for day-tripping—or even an overnight.

Levanto

Graced with a long, sandy beach, Levanto (LEH-vahn-toh) is packed in summer and popular with families, surfers, and beach bums. The rest of the year, it's just a small, sleepy town. Although not as charming as the Cinque Terre, Levanto is just a short train ride away and enjoys fewer crowds and more varied hotel and dining options, including budget-friendly family rooms and affordable apartments with kitchenettes. From Levanto you can bike or stroll on a delightful, level path to the uncrowded beach village of Bonassola and Framura, or spend a half-day on the no-wimps-allowed hike to Monterosso.

ORIENTATION TO LEVANTO

Levanto (pop. 5,200) faces the sea along a broad, curving beach. Much of the "new" town, closer to the train station, is actually old and full of character, with quaint pedestrian shopping streets like Via Garibaldi and handsome 19th-century villas close to the waterfront. The sleepy, twisty old town—bisected by a modern street—is tucked up against the adjacent hill.

Tourist Information
A Cinque Terre National Park info center is at the train station. The helpful TI is in the new town, at Piazza Cavour 1 (daily 9:00-13:00 & 15:00-18:00 except closed Sun afternoon, shorter hours off-season, +39 0187 808 125, www.visitlevanto.it).

Levanto

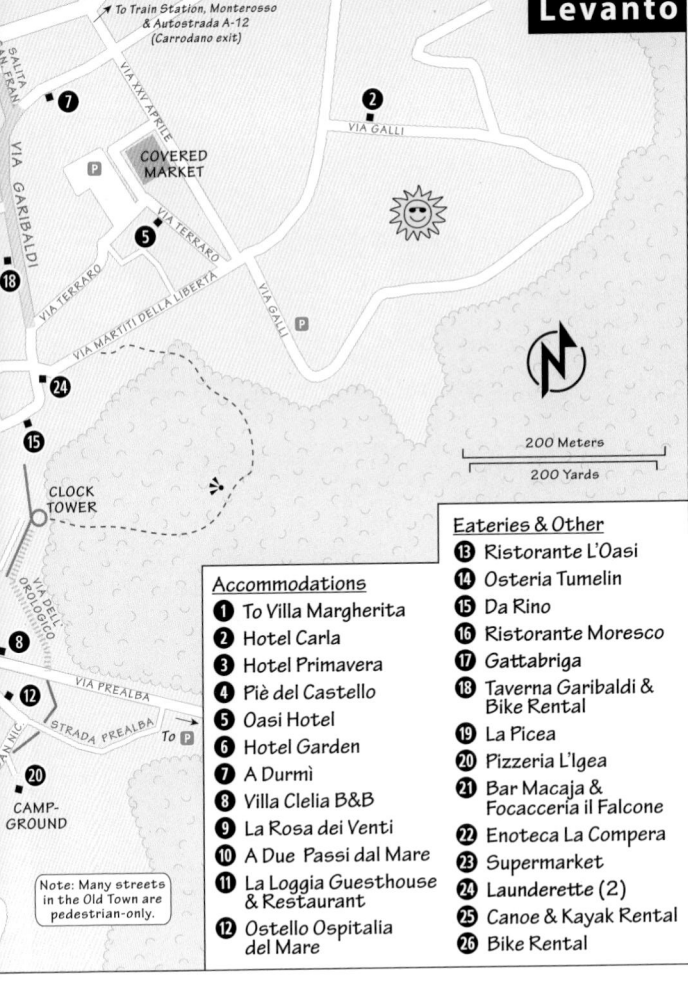

To Train Station, Monterosso & Autostrada A-12 (Carrodano exit)

VIA XXV APRILE
SALITA SAN FRAN
VIA GARIBALDI
COVERED MARKET
VIA TERRARO
VIA GALLI
VIA TERRARO
VIA MARTIRI DELLA LIBERTÀ
VIA GALLI
CLOCK TOWER
VIA DELL' OROLOGIO
VIA PREALBA
STRADA PREALBA
SAN NIC...
To P
CAMP-GROUND

Note: Many streets in the Old Town are pedestrian-only.

200 Meters
200 Yards

Accommodations

1 To Villa Margherita
2 Hotel Carla
3 Hotel Primavera
4 Piè del Castello
5 Oasi Hotel
6 Hotel Garden
7 A Durmì
8 Villa Clelia B&B
9 La Rosa dei Venti
10 A Due Passi dal Mare
11 La Loggia Guesthouse & Restaurant
12 Ostello Ospitalia del Mare

Eateries & Other

13 Ristorante L'Oasi
14 Osteria Tumelin
15 Da Rino
16 Ristorante Moresco
17 Gattabriga
18 Taverna Garibaldi & Bike Rental
19 La Picea
20 Pizzeria L'Igea
21 Bar Macaja & Focacceria il Falcone
22 Enoteca La Compera
23 Supermarket
24 Launderette (2)
25 Canoe & Kayak Rental
26 Bike Rental

Levanto's harbor is bordered by an elevated promenade.

Arrival in Levanto

By Train: From the train station (no baggage storage), head through the parking lot and down the stairs, turn right, and cross the bridge onto Corso Roma. The beach is straight ahead, and the town center, with most of my recommended hotels, restaurants, and the TI, is to your left. You can walk from the station to most of my listings in about 10 minutes.

By Car: If your hotel doesn't offer parking—or if you're not sleeping here—the lots surrounding the **train station** are affordable (€24/day) and handy for hopping a train to the Cinque Terre towns. If you're heading for the beach, the parking lot there is handy but more expensive.

Helpful Hints

Markets: Levanto's modern covered *mercato,* which sells produce and fish, is on Via XXV Aprile, between the train station and the beach (daily 7:30-13:00). On Wednesday morning, an **open-air market** with clothes, shoes, and housewares sets up along the beach.

Laundry: A **self-service launderette** stuffed with snack-and-drink vending machines is at Piazza Staglieno 38, facing an inviting park (daily 24 hours, +39 338 701 6341). A larger self-service place is at Via Garibaldi 32 (daily 8:00-22:00, same phone).

Sports Rentals: Right on the beach, **Rosa dei Venti** rents kayaks, canoes, surfboards, and windsurfing equipment (+39 329 451 1981, https://rosadeiventiboattours.com, Marco).

Bike Rental: Relatively flat Levanto, with light traffic, is a great bike town—and the ride to nearby Bonassola and Framura is easy and delightful. Regular bikes cost €10/day at both **Cicli Raso** (daily 9:30-12:30 & 15:00-19:00, closed Sun Nov-April, Via Garibaldi 63, +39 0187 802 511, www.cicliraso.com) and the **Sensafreni Bike Shop,** convenient to the beach boardwalk (daily 9:00-13:00 & 16:00-20:00, Piazza del Popolo 1, +39 0187 807 128).

E-Bike Tours: Ebikein offers a variety of guided tours on e-bikes. Options include a three-hour Levanto-Monterosso sunset tour (€59) and a four-hour trek to sanctuaries above the Cinque Terre towns (€65; +39 334 190 0496, https://ebikein-cinqueterre.it).

Boat Tours: Its base is in Monterosso, but **Sea Breeze** will pick you up in Levanto for full-day or *aperitivo* sunset tours. See page 45.

SIGHTS IN LEVANTO

Beach

Levanto's beach hides below a parking lot and promenade that's elevated above the sand—look for underpasses or stairs along its length. There are pretty boardwalks up on the elevated promenade and down along the beachfront. As you face the harbor, the boat dock is to your far left, and the diving center is to your far right.

In summer, three parts of the beach are free: both sides of the boat dock, and near Piazza Mazzini. The rest of the beach is broken up into private sections that you pay to enter. You can always stroll along the beach, even through the private sections—just don't sit down. Off-season, roughly October through May, the entire beach is free, and you can lay your towel anywhere you like. Ask your hotel for towels; most have beach towels to loan or rent.

Old Town

The old town spills down from the Church of Sant'Andrea (c. 1212), with Piazza del Popolo at its heart. Until a few decades ago, the town's open-air market was held at the 13th-century loggia (covered set of archways) in the square. The modern, elevated street is the old rail line (built in the 1870s and replaced by the current, higher route in 1970).

Explore the back streets (including Via Guani), the oratory of San Giacomo, and the old clock tower. Levanto was once an important harbor of the Republic of Genoa; from here, shipments of olive oil, wine, and the coveted red marble *rosso levanto* set sail.

▲Hike to Monterosso

This strenuous 3.5-hour hike is described in more detail on page 31. To begin in Levanto, start on Piazza del Popolo, and head uphill to the striped Church of Sant'Andrea. From the church courtyard, follow the sign to the *castello* (a private residence), go under the stone arch, and continue uphill. From here take trail SVA (following signs toward *Punta Mesco,* the rugged tip of the peninsula), then drop steeply down into Monterosso. (If you have knee issues, consider starting in Monterosso instead.)

▲Hike or Bike to Bonassola (and Framura)

Tucked along the main train line on a cove north of Levanto, the small beach resort of Bonassola (boh-nah-SOH-lah, pop. 950) is a peaceful little eddy. As far as Riviera beach resorts go, this is a jewel. With a low-key vibe, a tidy grid street plan that feels almost French, and a picturesque dark-sand beach hemmed in by jagged bluffs, Bonassola is a good alternative to the region's other beaches. And the next best thing to a beach day in Bonassola is getting there: A level, easy, rails-to-trails path cuts through the mountain from Levanto—enjoyable by foot, but even better by bike.

Levanto to Bonassola: Local **trains** run between Levanto and Bonassola (hourly, 3 minutes, confirm your train will stop in Bonassola). But I'd rather take the **promenade.** At the northern end of Levanto's beachfront road/parking lot, you'll find a level, roughly 1.5-mile path neatly divided into bike and pedestrian lanes. Most of the route is through well-lit former train tunnels, with brief breaks overlooking the sea (and hikes down to secluded beaches). The walk takes about 30 minutes, with long stretches through cool tunnels; by bike, it's less than 10 minutes. The promenade runs along the original rail line that linked Italy in the 1870s. Think of the effort of building it, and how much it meant for the newly unified country. The last trains chugged along the historic tracks in 1970, when the current rail line opened.

Visiting Bonassola: The town itself—with manicured prom-enades and piazzas—is worth exploring. **$$ Caffè delle Rose,** facing the town's elevated road (at Via Fratelli Rezzano 22), has good gelato, food, and drinks. Several *foccacerie* and other eateries cluster at the far end of town. The beach is separated from the town center by the elevated road (shared by bicyclists, walkers, and a parking lot). The inviting **beach** has mostly private sections, with a few free public areas.

Bonassola's seaside promenade

Framura's rocky harbor

Bonassola's beach is encircled by rocky bluffs.

For a scenic **walk/hike,** head to the far (north) end of the beach, where a promenade snakes along the base of the cliff (with rocky perches for sunbathing and swimming). For higher views, find the stairs near the flagpole, and follow the steps up on the right side of the yellow church. Popping out at the top, turn left along the scenic, private road as it curls around the top of the bay, with great views back on the town and beach; the path ends at the blocky little Madonnina della Punta chapel.

Bonassola to Framura (best for bicyclists): From Bonassola, the promenade continues another 1.5 miles to the town of **Framura**—a settlement made up of five medieval hamlets that rise from the seafront to the hilltop (pop. 750). Because this part of the route is almost entirely through tunnels, it's boring for walkers—but quick for bikers. The trail ends overlooking Framura's rocky little harbor and near its train station.

Visiting Framura: Park and lock your bike at the trailhead, take the stairs (or elevator) down to the small-boat harbor, cross under the train tracks through the boat-shed archway, walk through the big tunnel, and you'll emerge near the station. The welcoming **TI** at the Framura station has maps and advice (+39 0187 160 0577, www.framuraturismo.it).

At the station, the tunnel to platforms 2 and 3 also leads to the start of the scenic Via del Mare path, with a basic café at the trailhead. This easy promenade takes you north along a cliff face in 10 minutes to two small, pristine gravel beaches that are free and uncrowded.

SLEEPING IN LEVANTO

$$$ Villa Margherita is across the river and a bit uphill (about a 10-minute walk from the town center or train station), but the shaded view gardens, 12 colorfully tiled rooms, and tranquility are worth the walk (family rooms, air-con, elevator one flight up from street level, free parking, Via Trento e Trieste 31, +39 0187 807 212, mobile +39 328 842 6934, www.villamargherita.net, info@villamargherita.net, Paola).

$$$ Hotel Carla faces a school in a quiet residential zone, about 10 minutes from the beach and the station. Its 30 rooms come with contemporary style—most have balconies, and all are decorated in soothing, neutral colors (RS%, family rooms, air-con, elevator, free loaner bikes, Via Galli 3, +39 0187 808 275, mobile +39 351 52 3388, www.carlahotel.com, info@carlahotel.com, Laura).

$$$ Hotel Primavera is homey and family-run, with 17 colorful rooms—10 with balconies (but no views)—just a block from the beach (family rooms, request a quiet room off the street, includes hearty breakfast buffet, air-con, pay private parking, Via Cairoli 5, +39 0187 808 023, www.primaverahotel.com, info@primaverahotel.com; friendly Carlo, cheerful Daniela, and daughters Giuditta and Gloria).

$$$ Piè del Castello is right on the Levanto-Monterosso trail. Andrea and his wife, Tiziana, rent three double rooms, each with a patio and access to a sprawling garden with views of the ancient city wall and the Church of Sant'Andrea. Hikers will appreciate Andrea's knowledge of area trails (includes breakfast, air-con, fridge, free parking, Via Guido Semenza 2, +39 366 1467 7886, www.piedelcastello.com, info@piedelcastello.com).

$$$ Oasi Hotel, well-run by Silvia, has 14 rooms in a cozy small hotel behind the market hall. Some rooms have balconies, others have direct access to the garden, and a few have neither but are larger—request your choice when you reserve (RS%, air-con, elevator, pay parking, Via Terraro, +39 0187 807 356, www.oasihotel.eu, info@oasihotel.eu).

$$ Hotel Garden offers 17 functional, businesslike, modern rooms (all with balconies but no views) on the first floor of an apartment building. Its value is its proximity to the beach—just across the street (closed Nov-mid-March, air-con, elevator, free off-site parking, loaner bikes, Corso Italia 6, +39 0187 808 173, www.nuovogarden.com, info@nuovogarden.com, Davide and Damiano).

$$ A Durmì is a happy little guesthouse owned by lovely Graziella, Gianni, and their two daughters, Elisa and Chiara. Their sunny patios, green leafy gardens, six immaculate beach bungalow-type rooms, and five sunlit apartments make this a welcoming place to stay (breakfast extra, family rooms, air-con, bar, pay parking, Via D. Viviani 12, +39 0187 800 823, mobile +39 342 805 3135, www.adurmi.it, info@adurmi.it).

$$ Villa Clelia B&B offers six basic rooms with minifridges and terraces. The rooms surround a garden courtyard just a short walk up from the sea (in-room breakfast, air-con, pay parking, free loaner bikes; with the old town's loggia on your left, it's straight ahead at Piazza da Passano 1; +39 329 379 4859, www.villaclelia.it, info@villaclelia.it). Their apartments in the center economically sleep up to five.

$ La Rosa dei Venti is an affittacamere just a couple of blocks from the beach, in the old town. Enthusiastic Rosanna and her son Marco rent six old-fashioned rooms with dark hardwood floors, comfy rugs, and glittery seashore decor (air-con, parking, from Piazza del Popolo take the lane next to Osteria Tumelin to Via della Compera, +39 0187 808 165, mobile +39 328 742 8268, www.larosadeiventilevanto.com, info@larosadeiventilevanto.com).

$ A Due Passi dal Mare is along the town's main road, a five-minute walk from the beach or the train station. Friendly Francesca and husband Maurizio rent four crisp, quiet, ground-floor rooms in a large villa built by her grandfather in the 1920s, with access to a small back garden (free on-site parking, closed Jan-Feb, Corso Roma 37, +39 0187 809 177, mobile +39 338 960 1537, www.a2passidalmare.com, info@a2passidalmare.com).

$ La Loggia has eight cozy, older, and cheap rooms, perched above the old loggia on Piazza del Popolo (request balcony, quieter rooms in back, two basic side-by-side apartments great for families of 4-8, lots of stairs, air-con, free parking, reception open 9:00-23:00,

Piazza del Popolo 7, +39 0187 808 107, mobile +39 335 641 7701, www.loggialevanto.com, laloggialaloggia@gmail.com, Alessandro). They also have a recommended restaurant.

Hostel: A budget gem run by the city tourist association, ¢ **Ostello Ospitalia del Mare** has 70 basic beds, airy rooms, an elevator, and a terrace in a well-renovated medieval palazzo a few steps from the old town (all ages, dorms with private bath, private rooms, breakfast available, self-service laundry, no curfew or lockout; may close Nov-March, Via San Nicolò 1, +39 0187 802 562, www.ospitalialevanto.com, info@ospitalialevanto.com).

EATING IN LEVANTO

$$$$ Ristorante L'Oasi—spacious, bright, and with a garden feel right on the main square—is family run, with Claudio in the kitchen and Lella supervising the dining room. This is a polished setting for enjoying seafood, including fresh tuna tartare, marinated anchovies, and grilled swordfish (daily 12:30-14:30 & 19:30-22:30, closed Wed Sept-June, Piazza Cavour, +39 0187 800 856).

$$$ Osteria Tumelin has a dressy ambience in its elegant dining room, a casual covered terrace out front, and a wide selection of fresh seafood. Reservations are smart on weekends or to dine outside. Check out the aquarium containing giant lobster and moray eels in the corner dining room (daily 12:00-14:30 & 19:00-22:30, closed Thu, Via D. Grillo 32, across the square from the loggia, +39 0187 808 379, www.tumelin.it).

$$$ Da Rino, a small trattoria on a quiet pedestrian lane, dishes up seafood, meat, and homemade Ligurian specialties. Consider the grilled *totani* (squid), *pansotti con salsa di noci* (ravioli with walnut sauce), and *trofie al pesto* (pasta with pesto sauce). Dine indoors or out (Wed-Mon 18:30-22:00, closed Tue, Via Garibaldi 10, +39 0187 813 475).

$$ Ristorante la Loggia has been dishing up classic Ligurian cuisine for more than 50 years. Choose between the homey, wood-paneled dining room with nooks and crannies or the little terrace overlooking the square (daily 12:30-14:00 & 19:00-22:00, closed Wed and Nov-Feb, Piazza del Popolo 7, +39 0187 808 107). They also rent rooms (see previous section).

$$ Ristorante Moresco serves large portions of pasta and seafood at reasonable prices in a vaulted, candlelit room decorated with Moorish-style frescoes (Tue-Sun 12:00-14:00 & 19:00-21:00, closed Mon, reservations appreciated, Via Jacopo 24, +39 0187 807 253, Roberto and Francesca).

$$ Gattabriga hides out on a back lane behind Piazza del Popolo with a contemporary look; an updated and well-priced menu of pastas, seafood, and meats; and friendly service (Tue-Sun 19:00-21:30, closed Mon, Via Guani 47, +39 366 527 3582).

$$ Taverna Garibaldi, a comfy good-value place on the town's most characteristic street, serves focaccia with various toppings, made-to-order *farinata* (savory chickpea crêpes), salads, and more than 30 types of pizza (Fri-Wed 19:00-22:00, closed Thu, Via Garibaldi 57, +39 0187 808 098).

$$ La Picea offers creative wood-fired pizzas (check out the oven) and a large selection of beers—eat in or take out (Tue-Sun 12:00-14:30 & 18:30-23:00, closed Mon, just off Piazza Cavour at Via della Concia 18, +39 0187 802 063, mobile +39 392 958 3294).

$$ Pizzeria L'Igea is tucked inside the Campeggio Acquadolce campground, 50 yards past the hostel. It's a favorite among locals who know you don't have to be a camper to enjoy freshly made, budget-conscious pizza and pasta in their bright dining hall. Their specialty is *gattafin*—deep-fried herb-stuffed ravioli. Come early or be prepared to wait, even for takeout (daily 12:00-14:30 & 18:45-22:30, Via Guido Semenza 5, +39 0187 807 293).

$-$$ Bar Macaja, decorated in shabby-chic beach style, is a tiny place with a big happy vibe. Stop in for a continental breakfast, espresso, or a drink, *panini,* and local seafood—including anchovies prepared six ways (daily 7:00-23:00, just up from the beach at Via Cairoli 25, +39 349 844 8424).

$ Enoteca La Compera is a wine bar where you can try two wines and an *aperitivo* for €12. It offers a quiet respite on a hidden courtyard below the church in the old town (Thu-Tue 17:00-23:00, closed Wed, follow the red-brick road—under the stone arch—to Piazza della Compera 3, +39 334 712 8517).

Picnics and Bites on the Go: *Focaccerie, rosticcerie,* and delis with takeout pasta abound on Via Dante Alighieri. **$ Focacceria il Falcone** has a great selection of focaccia with different toppings, plus big salads (daily 9:30-22:00, shorter hours off-season, Via Cairoli 19, +39 0187 807 370). For more picnic options, try the *mercato* (see "Helpful Hints," earlier) or visit **Crai**, a good supermarket just off Piazza Cavour (daily 8:00-20:00 except Sun closed 13:00-15:00, Vicolo San Rocco 5). For a shaded setting, lay out your spread on a bench in the grassy park at triangular Piazza Staglieno. Another fine picnic spot is Piazza Cristoforo Colombo, located east of the swimming pool, with benches and sea views.

LEVANTO CONNECTIONS

Trains run frequently from Levanto to the Cinque Terre towns (5 minutes to Monterosso). A slower, more scenic, infrequent option is the **boat,** which stops at every Cinque Terre town (except Corniglia) before heading to Porto Venere (3/day in high season, price depends on distance traveled—or get a €37 all-day hop-on, hop-off ticket; only one return boat daily stops at Levanto, at about 18:50; get latest boat schedule and price sheet at TI or boat dock or check website, +39 0187 732 987, www.navigazionegolfodeipoeti.it).

Sestri Levante

Sestri Levante (SEH-stree leh-VAHN-teh) is squeezed as skinny as a hot dog between its two beaches. The pedestrian-friendly Via XXV Aprile, which runs down the middle of the peninsula, is lined with shops that sell takeout pizza, pastries, and beach paraphernalia.

Hans Christian Andersen enjoyed his visit here in the mid-1800s, writing, "What a fabulous evening I spent in Sestri Levante!" One of the bays—Baia delle Favole—is named in his honor (*favole* means "fairy tale"). The small mermaid curled on the edge of the fountain behind the TI is another nod to the beloved Danish storyteller.

ORIENTATION TO SESTRI LEVANTE

Sestri Levante (pop. 18,000) is dominated by its big, dull modern town in front of the train station. But don't be discouraged—the old-town peninsula, a 10-minute walk away, has charm to spare.

Tourist Information: It's at Corso Colombo 50, on the ground floor of Palazzo Fascie, the town's cultural center (daily 9:00-13:00 & 14:00-17:00, shorter hours off-season, +39 0185 478 530, www.sestri-levante.net). They can tell you about the summer bike-sharing program (€8/5 hours) and direct you to the trail (south of town) for a 1.5-hour hike (each way) to the scenic Punta Manara promontory.

Arrival in Sestri Levante: To reach the enjoyable pedestrian zone, the old-town peninsula, and beaches, follow the "Stroll the Town" advice next.

Baggage Storage: The tobacco store in the train station stores bags.

Market Day: It's on Saturday at Piazza Aldo Moro (8:00-13:00).

Laundry: A self-service launderette is in the urban zone southeast of the train station (daily 8:30-20:30, Via Costantino Raffo 8, +39 389 101 1454).

SIGHTS IN SESTRI LEVANTE

Stroll the Town

Head straight out from the train station and across the piazza to go down the arcaded Viale Roma until it dead ends at the leafy city park. Go left two blocks to the roundabout, and then take the second exit onto Corso Colombo (just past the Bermuda Bar). This main drag will take you to the TI before turning into the pedestrianized Via XXV Aprile. This street, running the length of the peninsula, is lively with shops, eateries, and delightful pastel facades. When you reach Piazza Matteotti, dominated by a large white Renaissance-era church, you'll have beaches to the right (pay) and left (free). If you continue up the lane to the left of the church, you'll pass a scenic amphitheater, then the evocative arches of a ruined chapel (bombed during World War II and left as a memorial). A few minutes farther on, past a stony Romanesque church, the road winds to the right to Grand Hotel dei Castelli. The rocky, forested bluff at the end of the town's peninsula is the huge private backyard of this fancy hotel.

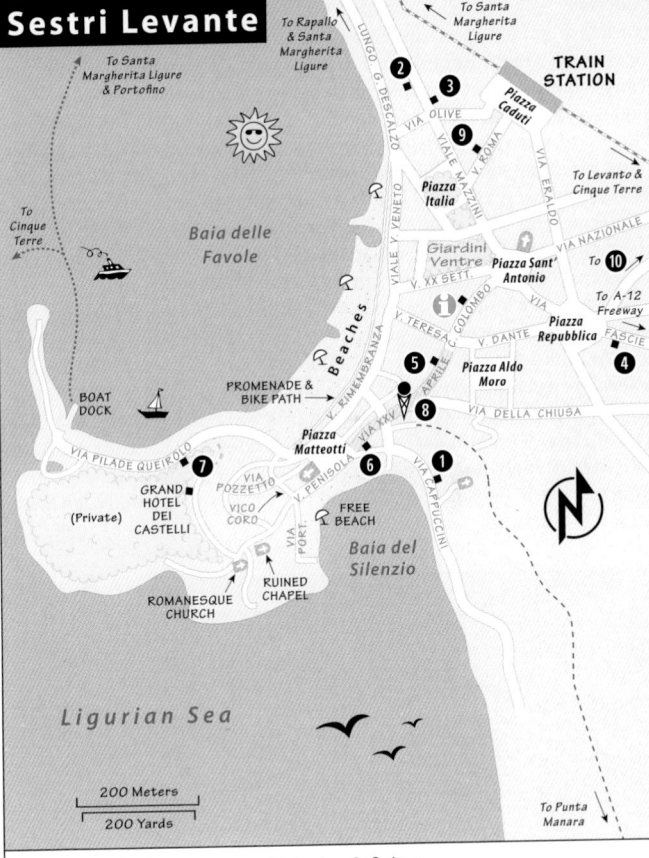

Sestri Levante

To Santa Margherita Ligure & Portofino

To Rapallo & Santa Margherita Ligure

To Santa Margherita Ligure

TRAIN STATION

Piazza Caduti

To Cinque Terre

Baia delle Favole

Beaches

Piazza Italia

Giardini Ventre

Piazza Sant' Antonio

To Levanto & Cinque Terre

To A-12 Freeway

Piazza Repubblica

Piazza Aldo Moro

PROMENADE & BIKE PATH

BOAT DOCK

VIA PILADE QUEIROLO

GRAND HOTEL DEI CASTELLI

(Private)

Piazza Matteotti

VIA POZZETTO

VICO CORO

FREE BEACH

Baia del Silenzio

ROMANESQUE CHURCH

RUINED CHAPEL

Ligurian Sea

200 Meters
200 Yards

To Punta Manara

Accommodations
1 Hotel Helvetia & Citto Beach Bar
2 Hotel Celeste
3 Hotel Genova
4 Albergo Marina

Eateries & Other
5 L'Osteria Mattana
6 Polpo Mario & Ristorante La Mainolla
7 Pelagica
8 Ice Cream's Angels
9 Supermarket
10 To Launderette

Beaches

These are named after the bays (*baie*) that they border. The less sce-nic, bigger beach, **Baia delle Favole,** is divided up much of the year (May-Sept) into sections that you must pay to enter. Fees, up to €30 per day in August, generally include chairs, umbrellas, and fewer crowds. There are several small free sections: at the ends and in the middle (look for *libere* signs, and ask *"Gratis?"* to make sure that it's free). For less expensive sections of beach (where you can rent a chair for about €8-10), ask for *spiaggia libera attrezzata* (spee-AH-jah LEE-behr-ah ah-treh-ZAHT-tah). The usual beach-town activities are clustered along this *baia:* boat rentals, sailing lessons, and bocce courts.

The town's other beach, **Baia del Silenzio,** is picturesque, nar-row, virtually all free, and jam-packed, providing a good chance to see Italian families at play. There isn't much more to do here than unroll a beach towel and join in. Because of the bay's small size and the cur-rents, the water gets warmer here than at Baia delle Favole. At the far end of Baia del Silenzio (under recommended Hotel Helvetia) is the **$$ Citto Beach Bar,** which offers front-row seats with bay views (summer until very late, spring and fall until sunset, sandwiches and salads at lunchtime only, Gilberto).

The Baia del Silenzio beach is ringed by bright, colorful cafés.

SLEEPING IN SESTRI LEVANTE

Hotels Genova and Celeste are the closest to the station. Either is an easy roll with wheeled luggage.

$$$$ Hotel Helvetia, overlooking Baia del Silenzio, feels posh and romantic, with 21 plush rooms, a large sun terrace with a heated, cliff-hanging swimming pool, and a peaceful garden atmosphere. With doubles renting for €400-plus in peak season, it's a big but enticing splurge (family rooms, air-con, elevator, valet parking, closed Nov-March, Via Cappuccini 43, +39 0185 41175, www.hotelhelvetia.it, helvetia@hotelhelvetia.it, Alex).

$$$ Hotel Celeste, a dream for beach lovers, rests along the waterfront. Its 39 rooms are modern, crisp, and pricey, but you're paying for the sea breeze (family rooms, air-con, elevator, attached beachside bar/breakfast terrace, Lungomare Descalzo 14, +39 0185 485 005, www.hotelceleste.com, info@hotelceleste.com, Franco).

$$ Hotel Genova, well run by the Bertoni family, has 19 shiny-clean, modern, and cheery rooms (three with sea views), a sunny lounge, a rooftop sundeck, and a good location just two blocks from Baia delle Favole (ask for quieter room in back, family rooms, air-con, elevator, pay parking, Viale Mazzini 126, +39 0185 41057, www.hotelgenovasestrilevante.com, info@hotelgenovasestrilevante.com, Stefano). They also book apartments in a nearby palazzo (www.appartamentisestrilevante.com).

$$ Albergo Marina's friendly Magda and her brother Santo rent 23 peaceful, clean, good-value rooms painted in sea-foam green. Though the hotel is on a busy boulevard in the more urban part of town, rooms face a quiet back courtyard and it's a short walk to the beach and train station (family rooms, air-con, elevator, free self-service laundry, pool table, closed Nov-Easter, Via Fascie 100, +39 0185 487 332, www.marinahotel.it, marinahotel@marinahotel.it).

EATING IN SESTRI LEVANTE

Via XXV Aprile abounds with pastry shops, bakeries selling takeout pizza by the slice, and other edibles. For picnics, stop by a supermarket on your way from the train station; you'll pass a Carrefour Express at

Viale Roma 25 (open daily). For a sit-down meal, try one of the following places.

$$ L'Osteria Mattana has long, shared tables in two white-tiled dining rooms (one in front and the other past the wood oven and brazier). Daily specials—most featuring seafood—are listed on chalkboard menus (lunch Sat-Sun only 12:30-14:30, dinner daily 19:30-22:30, closed Mon, Via XXV Aprile 34, +39 0185 457 633, Marco).

$$$ Polpo Mario has its own boat that brings in fresh fish each day. This is the place to try *polpo* (octopus), either spicy (*alla diavola*) or as *ragù di polpo* tossed with spaghetti. For an appetizer, the *acciughe al limone*—fresh anchovies cured in lemon—might just change your mind about this humble fish (Tue-Sun 12:00-15:00 & 19:00-23:00, closed Mon, reservations smart, Via XXV Aprile 163, +39 0185 480 203, www.polpomario.com).

$$$ Pelagica, a contemporary restaurant with a choice spot overlooking the Baia delle Favole, focuses on seafood, from anchovies to fried squid to traditional fish soup. Their rooftop terrace doubles as a cocktail lounge in the evening (kitchen daily 12:00-14:15 & 19:00-22:15, closed Wed, Via Pilade Queirolo 7, +39 393 882 0255).

$$ Ristorante La Mainolla offers pizzas, big salads, focaccia sandwiches, and reasonably priced pastas near Piazza Matteotti (daily 12:00-16:00 & 19:00-22:00, Via XXV Aprile 187, +39 0185 42792).

Gelato: Tourists flock to **Ice Cream's Angels,** flamboyantly set at the intersection of Via XXV Aprile and Via della Chiusa. Riccardo and Elena artfully load up your cone and top it with a dollop of Nutella chocolate-hazelnut cream (daily until late in summer).

SESTRI LEVANTE CONNECTIONS

From Sestri Levante by Train to: Levanto (at least hourly, 15-30 minutes), **Monterosso** (at least hourly, 30-40 minutes), **other Cinque Terre towns** (nearly hourly direct, more with a change in Levanto or Monterosso), **Santa Margherita Ligure** (2/hour, 20-25 minutes).

Boats depart to the Cinque Terre, Porto Venere, Santa Margherita Ligure, Portofino, and San Fruttuoso from the dock (*molo*) on the peninsula (Easter-Oct, +39 0185 284 670, www.traghettiportofino.it).

Santa Margherita Ligure

If you need the Riviera of movie stars, park your yacht at Portofino. Or you can settle down with more elbow room in nearby and more personable Santa Margherita Ligure (SAHN-tah mar-geh-REE-tah lee-GOO-reh), one hour by train from the Cinque Terre.

On a quick day trip to Santa Margherita Ligure, walk the beach promenade and see the old town center before catching the bus or boat to Portofino to discover what all the fuss is about. With more time, Santa Margherita Ligure (pop. 10,200) makes a fine overnight stop or a home base for visiting the Cinque Terre.

ORIENTATION TO SANTA MARGHERITA LIGURE

Santa Margherita Ligure tumbles easily downhill from its train station. The town has a fun Old World resort character and a breezy harborfront with a beach promenade. With its nice big-city vitality, it feels bustling and lived-in, even off-season.

Tourist Information: The TI is as central as can be, in a green harborside kiosk at the city traffic hub, Piazza Vittorio Veneto (daily 9:30-13:00 & 15:00-17:00, shorter hours off-season, +39 0185 28 74 85, www.livesanta.it). They sell tickets for bus #782 to Portofino, which stops at the curb in front.

Arrival in Santa Margherita Ligure

By Train: The bar/café (at the end of track 1) stores bags (small fee) and sells bus, train, and sightseeing-boat tickets. Bus #782 to Portofino leaves from in front of the station.

To get from the station to the city center, take the stairs marked *Mare* (sea) down to the harbor; or turn right and head more gently down Via Roma, which leads to the town center, the TI, the start of my town walk, and recommended hotels (about 10 minutes away on foot).

By Car: Ask your hotelier about parking; some have free spots. Otherwise, try a private pay lot such as the Garage Europa *autopark* next to the post office (Via Roma 38). An hourly pay-and-display lot is by the harbor, in front of the fish market. Parking is generally free

Santa Margherita Ligure spills down the hill to its sunny waterfront promenade.

where there are white lines (though there may be a time limit); blue lines mean you pay.

Helpful Hints

Market: A market sets up on Fridays on Corso Matteotti (8:00-13:00).

Laundry: There's none in town.

Bike Rental: City and e-bikes are available to rent by the day from **Ciclomania,** which puts together guided day trips to nearby destinations, too (Mon-Sat 8:30-12:30 & 15:30-19:00, closed Sun, Via Luigi Bozzo 22, +39 0185 283 530, www.ciclomania-liguria. it, Mimmo).

Scooter Rental: Head to **GM Rent,** which also has little Smart cars in its fleet (daily 9:00-13:00 & 15:00-19:00, Via XXV Aprile 11, +39 329 406 6274, www.gmrent.it, Francesco).

Taxi: Taxis wait outside the train station and TI and charge €15 for a ride anywhere in town, €25 to Paraggi beach, and €35 to Portofino (+39 0185 286 508).

Driver: Helpful taxi driver **Alessandro** has cars and minivans, and offers airport transfers to Genoa, Milan, Florence, and Nice. He also leads local excursions, including day trips to the Cinque Terre (+39 338 860 2349, www.alessandrotaxi.com, alessandrotaxi@ yahoo.it).

SANTA MARGHERITA LIGURE WALK

Get your bearings with this self-guided walk, starting on Piazza Caprera, the square facing the exuberant Baroque facade of the Basilica of Santa Margherita.

Basilica of Santa Margherita

The town's main church is textbook Italian Baroque (free, daily 7:30-12:00 & 15:00-18:30). Its 18th-century facade hides a 17th-century interior slathered with art and dripping with chandeliers. The altar is typical of 17th-century Ligurian altars—shaped like a boat, with lots of shelf space for candles, flowers, and relics. Its centerpiece is a much-venerated statue of Our Lady of the Rose that's adorned this altar since 1756.

Baroque is theater...and this altar is stagecraft. After the

The town has pedestrian-friendly squares...

...and an impressive church.

Vatican II decrees of the 1960s, priests began to face their flocks instead of the old altars. For this reason, all over the Catholic world, modern tables serving as post-Vatican II altars stand in front of earlier altars, like the one here, that are no longer the center of attention during Mass.

Wander the church and its chapels, noticing the inlaid-marble floors and sparkling glass chandeliers. As you marvel at the richness, remember that the region's aristocrats amassed wealth from trade from the 11th to the 15th century. When Constantinople fell to the Turks in 1453, free trade in the Mediterranean stopped, and Genovese traders became bankers—making even more money. A popular saying of the day was, "Silver is born in America, lives in Spain, and dies in Genoa." Bankers here served Spain's 17th-century royalty and aristocracy, and their accrued wealth paid for the art you see here.

Piazza Caprera

Each day this square hosts a few farmers selling their produce. On the corner of Via Cavour, just next to the basilica, don't miss **Seghezzo,** a venerable luxury grocery store that's a feast for the eyes. If you don't go in, at least admire the window displays.

▶ *Now side-trip up the town's main corridor of retail commerce, Via Palestro and Via Cavour. You'll go two blocks up to Piazza Mazzini and back.*

Main Shopping Streets

Via Cavour and Via Palestro are parallel streets divided by very tall, narrow buildings. As you head up Via Cavour (on the left, by

Seghezzo grocery), check out the shops on the right: The buildings that separate Via Cavour from Via Palestro are so skinny you see right through to the other side. The mix of fine boutiques, wine bars, jewelers, and casual restaurants hints at the elite—but not flashy—ambience of the town.

In two blocks you'll emerge onto a square, Piazza Mazzini, with enough elbow room to study the pastel house fronts. These facades were painted and decorated in the characteristic Ligurian trompel'oeil style from the turn of the last century. Every building presents some sort of illusion—the decorators went so far as to add painted-on upper windows, shutters, and window frames.

Now do a U-turn onto Via Palestro to return to where we started (staying straight past the recommended **Angolo 48** restaurant on the corner). At #34 (on the left) you'll pass a traditional *panificio* (bakery) where you can say, *"Vorrei un etto di focaccia"* to treat yourself to about a quarter-pound of the region's famed bread. Just beyond, on the right at #13, **Fruttivendolo "Milanese"** is one of the many greengrocers in town selling an array of tempting produce and glass-jarred delicacies.

▶ *Back on Piazza Caprera, turn left and walk away from the church one block to busy Largo Antonio Giusti. Across the street, a penguin marks the recommended Gelateria Centrale. Head right to Piazza Vittorio Veneto, with its busy roundabout and little park on the harbor, where you'll find the TI (which sells bus tickets) and a bus stop for Portofino. Use the crosswalks to reach the promenade.*

Beachfront Promenade

Take a look to the left, along Viale Andrea Doria. The sidewalk is wider than the street, reflecting how visitors have promenaded here, under pastel facades, for more than a century. Now turn right and walk into the waterfront park.

At the midpoint of the park is a Christopher Columbus statue. He was born "Cristoforo Colombo" in 1451 in Genoa, near here, and first sailed on Genovese boats along this Ligurian coast. Next comes a statue of King Victor Emmanuel II, always ready to brandish his sword and create Italy.

▶ *Head out on the little pier with the white statue facing out to sea.*

Santa Margherita Ligure

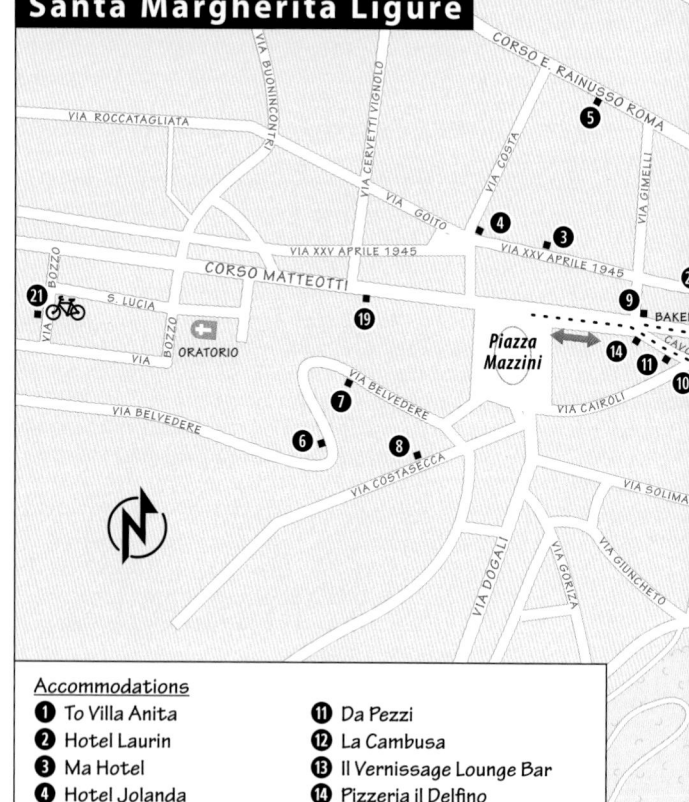

Accommodations

1. To Villa Anita
2. Hotel Laurin
3. Ma Hotel
4. Hotel Jolanda
5. Hotel Tigullio et de Milan
6. Hotel Sant'Andrea
7. Sabini Rentals
8. Albergo Annabella

Eateries & Other

9. Angolo 48
10. Vineria Machiavello
11. Da Pezzi
12. La Cambusa
13. Il Vernissage Lounge Bar
14. Pizzeria il Delfino
15. Pizzeria Cavaliere
16. Simonetti Gelateria
17. Gelateria Centrale
18. Seghezzo Grocery
19. Supermarket
20. Fruttivendolo "Milanese"
21. Bike Rental
22. Scooter & Smart Car Rental

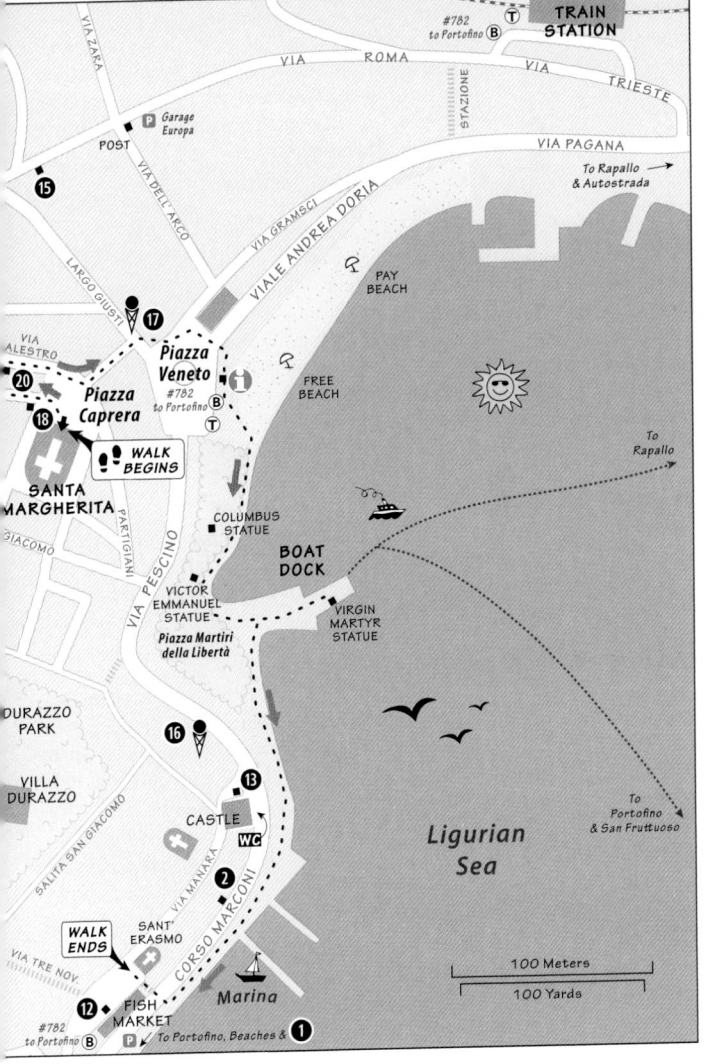

TRAIN
STATION

#782
to Portofino Ⓑ Ⓣ

VIA ZARA

VIA ROMA

VIA TRIESTE

Garage
Europa

POST

VIA PAGANA

STAZIONE

VIA DELL'ARCO

VIA GRAMSCI

VIALE ANDREA DORIA

To Rapallo
& Autostrada

⑮

LARGO GIUSTI

PAY
BEACH

⑰

*Piazza
Veneto*

#782
to Portofino Ⓑ

FREE
BEACH

VIA
ALESTRO

⑳

⑱

*Piazza
Caprera*

Ⓣ

👣 **WALK
BEGINS**

To
Rapallo

**SANTA
MARGHERITA**

GIACOMO

VIA PESCINO

VIA PARTIGIANI

COLUMBUS
STATUE

**BOAT
DOCK**

VICTOR
EMMANUEL
STATUE

VIRGIN
MARTYR
STATUE

*Piazza Martiri
della Libertà*

**DURAZZO
PARK**

⑯

**VILLA
DURAZZO**

SALITA SAN GIACOMO

⑬

VIA MANARA

CASTLE

WC

*Ligurian
Sea*

②

CORSO MARCONI

**WALK
ENDS**

SANT'
ERASMO

To
Portofino
& San Fruttuoso

VIA TRE NOV.

100 Meters

100 Yards

⑫

**FISH
MARKET**

Marina

#782
to Portofino Ⓑ

Ⓟ To Portofino, Beaches &

①

View from the Pier

From here, standing with the "Santa Margherita Virgin Martyr" statue, you can take in all of Santa Margherita Ligure—from the villas dotting the hills, to the castle built in the 16th century to defend against pirates, to the exclusive hotels. Tourist boats to Portofino, the Cinque Terre, and beyond depart from this pier.

▶ *Continue along the waterfront on Corso Marconi.*

Harbor and Fish Market

On the right, notice the trendy, recommended **Il Vernissage Lounge Bar** with tables up at the base of the castle (with WCs down below). Continuing around the corner from the castle (closed to visitors), walk along the harbor. The region's largest fishing fleet—20 boats—ties up here. The fishing industry survives, drag-netting octopus, shrimp, and miscellaneous "blue fish." The **fish market** (Mercato del Pesca, across the street, inside the rust-colored building with arches and columns) wiggles weekdays from about 16:00 until 20:00 or so—depending on who's catching what and when. It's a cool scene as fishermen take bins of freshly caught fish directly to waiting customers.

▶ *Climb the narrow brick stairs just to the right of the fish market to a delightful little square. Find the characteristic, black-and-white pebble mosaic and relax on the benches to enjoy harbor views. Facing the square is the little...*

Oratory of Sant'Erasmo

Named for St. Erasmus, the protector of sailors, this building is an "oratory," where a brotherhood of faithful men who did anonymous good deeds congregated and worshipped. Although it's rarely open, do check. The interior is decorated with ships and paintings of storms that local seafarers survived—thanks to St. Erasmus. The huge crosses standing in the nave are carried through town on special religious holidays.

▶ *Your walk is over. For a little extra exercise to see a pleasant park, climb the long stairs from here up to the Church of San Giacomo (with an interior similar to the Basilica of Santa Margherita) and Durazzo Park.*

SIGHTS IN SANTA MARGHERITA LIGURE

Durazzo Park (Parco di Villa Durazzo)

This park is a delight, with a breezy café (seasonal), a carefully coiffed Italian garden, and an intentionally wild "English garden" below (free, daily 9:00-19:00, July-Aug until 20:00, closes earlier off-season, WC near café). The Italian garden is famous for its varied collection of palm trees and an extensive collection of camellias. It's OK to feed the large turtles in the central pond (they like bits of fish or meat).

The park is dominated by **Villa Durazzo.** It's not worth touring for most, but its remarkable pebble courtyard, carpeted in a fleur-de-lis pattern of white and gray stone, deserves a look.

Beaches (Spiagge)

The handiest free beaches are just below the train station toward the boat dock. But the best beaches are on the road to Portofino. These beaches are a 20-minute walk from downtown, or you can take bus #782 from the train station or from in front of the TI at Piazza Veneto.

The beach on the south side of **Grand Hotel Miramare** offers a relaxing experience and is good for kids. Also nice is **Minaglia,**

Enjoying a sunny day on one of Santa Margherita Ligure's beaches.

with rentable sunbeds and kayaks. My favorite, **Giò e Rino** (just before the Covo di Nord Est night club), has sunbeds for rent and a fun, youthful crowd.

Paraggi, a small, sandy beach halfway to Portofino (and an easy stop on the bus #782 route), is better than any of the close-in Santa Margherita Ligure beaches, but it's pricey (as much as €60/day in July and Aug)—and it can be packed with sun worshippers from Portofino (where there's no beach—only rocks). There's more than one *bagni* establishment here, so choose the one that most appeals. Off-season, the entire beach is all yours and free. A narrow patch of sand smack-dab in the middle of Paraggi beach is free year-round.

SLEEPING IN SANTA MARGHERITA LIGURE

Except for Villa Anita, all the hotels listed here are within a 10-minute walk of the train station.

$$$$ Villa Anita is an elegant-yet-homey family hotel run by Daniela and her son, Sandro. They rent 12 tidy rooms—nearly all with terraces—overlooking a peaceful residential neighborhood a five-minute uphill walk from the seaside boulevard (air-con, family rooms, playground, small gym, small heated pool and sauna, loaner bikes, scooter and boat rentals, pay parking, closed in winter, Viale Minerva 25, +39 0185 286 543, www.hotelvillaanita.com, info@hotelvillaanita.com).

$$$$ Hotel Laurin, nestled up against castle ruins, offers 44 slick, modern, and pricey rooms looking onto the sea. All double rooms face the harbor and have terraces; on the rooftop sundeck, there's a small pool (RS%, air-con, elevator, gym, limited pay parking—request when you reserve, just past the castle at Corso Marconi 3, +39 0185 289 971, www.laurinhotel.it, info@laurinhotel.it, Tiziana).

$$$ Ma Hotel is a crystal-chandelier-classy boutique hotel with a fresh, modern flair. Although it sits along a busy street, its 11 stylish and spacious rooms are at the back of the building (air-con, patio, free minibar, Via XXV Aprile 18, +39 0185 280 224, www.mahotel.it, info@mahotel.it, Matteo).

$$$ Pastine Hotels is a chain of three well-run hotels that combine solid service, sumptuous public spaces, and pleasant rooms. The two main branches are around the corner from each other, an easy walk from the station: **Hotel Jolanda** has a lavish lobby and regal colors, and its 49 pleasant rooms have soothing decor (RS%, air-con, elevator, free use of small weight room and hot tub, pay dry sauna, valet parking, Via Luisito Costa 6, +39 0185 287 512, www.hoteljolanda. it, info@hoteljolanda.it). **Hotel Tigullio et de Milan** is smaller and tidier, with 36 updated rooms. The superior rooms are especially nice, but even most standard doubles come with a terrace—specify when you book. The rooftop sun terrace offers sunbeds, a bar, and a hot tub in the summer (RS%, air-con, elevator, valet parking, Via Rainusso 3, +39 0185 287 455, www.hoteltigullio.eu, info@hoteltigullio.eu). The newest branch, the boutique-like **Hotel Sant'Andrea,** has 11 rooms just above Piazza Mazzini, with a patio and whirlpool for guests (RS%, air-con, valet parking, Via Belvedere 10, +39 0185 293 487, www. hotelsantandrea.net, info@hotelsantandrea.net).

$$ Sabini Rentals, in a bland but central residential zone, offers three straightforward rooms and one apartment with a tiny corner kitchen (RS%, family rooms, 2-night minimum, cash only, breakfast on request, laundry service, Via Belvedere 31, +39 338 902 7582, www. sabinirentals.com, info@sabinirentals.com, Cristina and Giancarlo).

$ Albergo Annabella has 11 well-kept rooms, six of which are old-style budget throwbacks with sinks in the room and shared bath (no breakfast, air-con, Via Costasecca 10, +39 0185 286 531, www. albergoannabella.it, info@albergoannabella.it, Annabella speaks just enough English).

EATING IN SANTA MARGHERITA LIGURE

In the City Center

$$$ Angolo 48, run by savvy Elisa and Valentina, serves well-presented and reasonably priced Genovese and Ligurian dishes. This cozy locale is popular: Either arrive right when they open or make a reservation. There's great seating both on the square and inside. Try their handmade *pansotti* in walnut sauce (lunch Sat-Sun only 12:00-13:45, dinner Tue-Sun 18:30-22:00, closed Mon, Via Palestro 48, +39 0185 286 650).

$$ Vineria Machiavello feels more urban Tuscan than seaside Ligurian. This well-stocked *enoteca* (wine shop) offers tastings and full bottles, but also serves a short menu of well-priced dishes at a few humble tables tucked between the wine racks (Wed-Mon 10:00-14:00

& 17:30-24:00, closed Tue, in the heart of the pedestrian zone at Via Cavour 17, +39 0185 286 122).

$ Da Pezzi, with a cheap cafeteria-style atmosphere, is packed with locals at midday and at night. They're standing at the bar munching *farinata* (crêpes made from chickpeas, available Oct-May 18:00-20:00) or enjoying pesto and fresh fish in the dining room. Consider the deli counter with its Genovese picnic ingredients (Sun-Fri 10:00-14:00 & 18:00-21:00, table service after 12:00 and 18:15, closed Sat, Via Cavour 21, +39 0185 285 303, Giancarlo and Giobatta).

On the Waterfront

All along the harbor side of Via Tommaso Bottaro, south of the marina, you'll find restaurants, pizzerias, and bars serving food with a nautical view.

$$$ La Cambusa, perched above the fish market, is popular for its seafood. While the food is forgettable, the view from its harborside terrace is not. In cooler weather, the terrace is covered and heated. Diners receive a free glass of *sciacchetrà* (dessert wine) and biscotti with this book (daily 12:00-15:00 & 19:00-23:00 except closed Thu Oct-June, Via Tommaso Bottaro 1, +39 0185 287 410).

At **$$ Il Vernissage Lounge Bar,** you can nurse your drink with a million-dollar view. There are 20 wines by the glass, plus cocktails and *spritzes,* which come with a nice plate of finger food (daily 18:00-late, Sun from 11:00, Salita al Castello 8, +39 349 220 5846, Sandro).

Budget Options

$$ Pizzeria il Delfino serves thin, big, wood-fired pizzas in a rustic, fun local scene, with a few quiet tables outside and tight inside seating under nautical bric-a-brac (cash only, daily 12:00-15:00 & 18:00-23:00 except closed Tue lunch, Via Cavour 29, +39 0185 286 488). For cheaper takeout pizza and kebabs, head for **Pizzeria Cavaliere,** on the way to the station (open daily, Via Roma 16).

Gelato: Along the waterfront, try **Simonetti**—especially their chocolate-truffle *tartufato* (under the castle at Piazza Martiri della Libertà 48). **Gelateria Centrale,** just off Piazza Veneto near the cinema, serves up *pinguino* (penguin) cones, your choice of gelato dipped in chocolate (Largo Antonio Giusti 14).

Groceries: Classy **Seghezzo** is a gorgeous luxury grocery, deli, and wine shop. It's great for a meal to go—ask them to *riscaldare* (heat up) their white *lasagne* al pesto or dish up their special *carpaccio di polpo*—thinly sliced octopus (Thu-Tue 7:30-13:00 & 15:30-20:00, closed Wed off-season, near the church on Via Cavour, +39 0185 287 172, www.seghezzo.com). Cheaper and less romantic, the **Co-op** grocery is a good place to stock up (daily 8:00-13:30 & 15:30-19:30 except Sun from 8:30, Corso Giacomo Matteotti 9).

SANTA MARGHERITA LIGURE CONNECTIONS

To reach the **Cinque Terre** towns (beyond Monterosso), you'll usually have to change in Sestri Levante, Levanto, or Monterosso.

From Santa Margherita Ligure by Train to: Sestri Levante (2/ hour, 20-25 minutes), **Monterosso** (at least hourly, 50-60 minutes, often with a change in Sestri Levante), **La Spezia** (nearly hourly direct, 55-65 minutes), **Pisa** (5/day direct, 2 hours, more with transfer), **Florence** (4 hours, transfer in La Spezia or Pisa), **Milan** (9/day direct, 2 hours, more with transfer in Genoa), **Ventimiglia**/French border (almost hourly, 3.5 hours, change in Genoa), **Venice** (5-7 hours, 1-2 changes).

By Boat to the Cinque Terre: Tour boats make various trips to Vernazza, Porto Venere, and other ports nearly every day. Pick up a schedule of departures and excursion options from the TI, visit the ticket shack on the dock, call +39 0185 284 670, or check www. traghettiportofino.it.

Portofino

Santa Margherita Ligure, with its aristocratic architecture, hints at old wealth. But nearby Portofino (pop. 500)—with its sleek jewelry shops, art galleries, and haute couture boutiques filling a humble village shell—has the sheen of new money. It's the kind of place where the sailing masts are taller than the houses and church steeples. But the picture-perfect harbor, classic Italian architecture, and wooded peninsula turn posh Portofino into an appealing destination. Just a couple of miles down the coast, it's a fun, easy day trip from Santa Margherita Ligure.

Popular with celebrities, Portofino is a classic Riviera beach town: pricey and pretty.

Planning Your Time: In summer, my favorite Portofino plan is to visit in the late afternoon. Leave Santa Margherita Ligure by bus at about 16:30, get off at Paraggi beach, and hike 30 minutes over the bluff into Portofino. Explore the town, splurge for a drink on the harborfront, or get a takeout fruity sundae (*paciugo*; pah-CHOO-goh) and sit by the water. Then return by bus to Santa Margherita Ligure for dinner (confirm late departures). If you plan to do longer hikes around Portofino, come earlier in the day.

Tourist Information: The TI is tucked under an arch between the harbor and the bus stop (Wed-Mon 10:00-13:00 & 14:00-18:00, closed Tue, Via Roma 35, +39 0185 215 037, www.comune.portofino.genova.it).

GETTING TO PORTOFINO

You can reach Portofino from Santa Margherita Ligure by bus or boat, or on foot. For a fun combination, go one way by bus and on foot from Paraggi, and the other way by boat. (I wouldn't suggest biking it, because of the blind corners.)

By Bus: Catch bus #782 from Santa Margherita Ligure's train station, TI, or bus stops along the harbor (€3 one-way or €5 round-trip,

€1 more if bought from driver, 4/hour, 20 minutes, www.amt.genova. it). Buy tickets at the train station bar, the green ticket machine outside the TI, or any newsstand, tobacco shop, or shop that displays a *Biglietti Bus* sign. If you're at the TI, grab a bus schedule to plan your return (last bus around 24:00 in summer).

By Taxi: A taxi ride from Santa Margherita Ligure costs around €35 to Portofino or €25 to Paraggi beach (more at night). Taxi stands in Santa Margherita Ligure are at the train station and at the curb in front of the TI.

By Boat: The boat makes the 15-minute trip with more class and scenery—and without the traffic jams. The dock in Santa Margherita Ligure juts out from the waterfront park at Piazza Martiri della Libertà, near the TI (€8 one-way, €14 round-trip; hourly departures May-Sept daily 10:15-16:15, fewer in April and Oct, no boats off-season; purchase tickets at the dock, +39 0185 284 670, www.traghettiportofino.it).

If you arrive in Portofino by boat but will be busing back, follow the narrow lanes up from the harbor to the bus stop in Piazza della Libertà (ticket machine and tobacco store there sell tickets).

On Foot: To hike from Santa Margherita Ligure to Portofino, you have two options: You can follow the sidewalk along (and sometimes hanging over) the sea (1 hour, 2.5 miles)—although traffic can be noisy, and in places, the footpath disappears. Or, if you're hardy and ambitious, you can take a quieter two-hour hike by leaving Santa Margherita Ligure at Via Maragliano, then following the Ligurian-symbol trail markers (keep a close eye out for red-and-white stripes). This hike takes you high into the hills. Keep left after Cappelletta delle Gave. Several blocks past a castle, you'll drop down into Paraggi beach, where you'll take the Portofino trail (described next) the rest of the way.

Bus-and-Hike Option: For a short—but rewarding—30-minute hike into Portofino, ride bus #782 from Santa Margherita Ligure to Paraggi beach (tell the driver you want to get off there—you can't miss the inlet bay with a sandy beach). At the Portofino end of the beach, look for the *Parco di Portofino* sign to find the steps that begin the hilly, paved trail marked *Pedonale per Portofino* high above the road. There's a fair amount of up and down, but it's all well-paved and scenic. After Paraggi you'll curl around another bay—with the famously top-end Hotel Splendido hovering on the hill above—before snaking your way to Portofino.

SIGHTS IN PORTOFINO

▲▲Self-Guided Visual Tour from the Harbor

Stand or sit on the angled boat launch where Piazza Martiri dell'Olivetta meets the harbor (or nurse an overpriced cocktail at the nearby café tables) and get oriented to Portofino. It's one of the Mediterranean's most beautiful and famous little resorts.

Scanning the narrow pastel houses around the harbor, notice the painted-on details. You may also see laundry hanging out to dry—a surprising reminder that, while Ferragamo and Prada may reside on street level, actual villagers still live upstairs.

Now look out to the well-protected natural harbor, which has held substantial strategic value ever since the Romans first founded a town here. Since then, it has been appreciated by everyone from Napoleon to the Nazis.

A new flock of fans arrived in the 1950s, when *National Geographic* ran a beautiful article on the idyllic port. Locals claim that's when the Hollywood elite took note. Liz Taylor and Richard Burton came here annually (as did Liz Taylor and Eddie Fisher). During one famous party, Rex Harrison dropped his Oscar into the bay (it was recovered). Ava Gardner came down from her villa each evening for a drink—sporting her famous fur coat. Greta Garbo loved to swim naked in the harbor, not knowing (or caring) that half the town was watching. Truman Capote also called Portofino home. But VIPs were also here a century earlier. Friedrich Nietzsche famously wrote about philosophizing with the mythical prophet Zarathustra on the path between Portofino and Santa Margherita Ligure.

Today, the celebrity cachet lives on. When you tell locals you're going to Portofino, they say, "Maybe you'll see George and Amal Clooney!" Count the yachts and the tall-masted sailboats and imagine who might be on them.

Now scan the panorama on the hillside in front of you. On the left is **Castello Brown,** an actual medieval castle built by the Genovese in the 16th century to protect this strategic harbor. It later became a private mansion, and today it is primarily an event space featuring lush gardens and sweeping viewpoints (€5; daily July-Aug 10:00-20:00, March-June until 19:00, shorter hours in fall and winter, +39 375 791 8926, www.castellobrown.com).

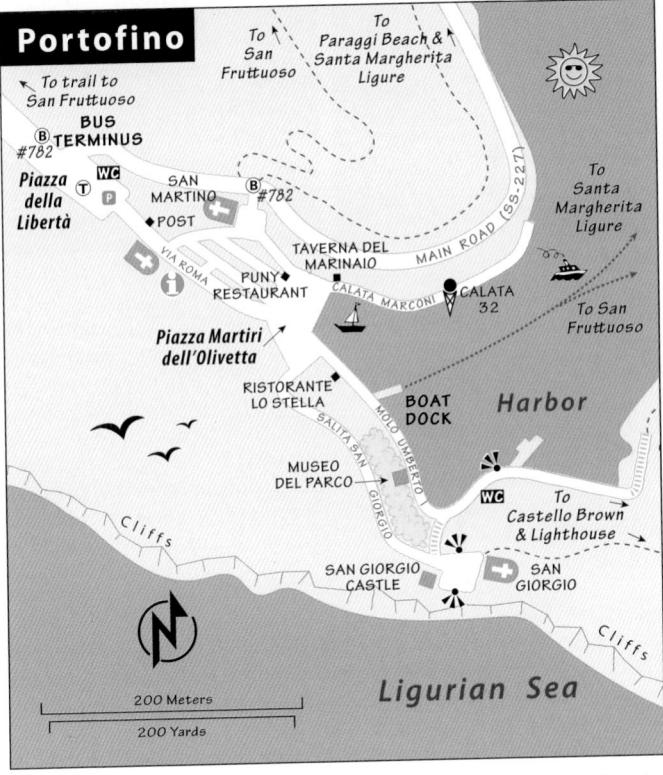

Portofino

To trail to San Fruttuoso

To San Fruttuoso

To Paraggi Beach & Santa Margherita Ligure

Ⓑ **BUS TERMINUS** #782

Piazza della Libertà

WC

Ⓣ P POST

SAN MARTINO

Ⓑ #782

VIA ROMA

PUNY RESTAURANT

TAVERNA DEL MARINAIO

MAIN ROAD (SS-227)

CALATA MARCONI

CALATA 32

To Santa Margherita Ligure

To San Fruttuoso

Piazza Martiri dell'Olivetta

RISTORANTE LO STELLA

SALITA SAN GIORGIO

MOLO UMBERTO

BOAT DOCK

Harbor

MUSEO DEL PARCO

WC

To Castello Brown & Lighthouse

Cliffs

SAN GIORGIO CASTLE

SAN GIORGIO

N

Cliffs

Ligurian Sea

200 Meters

200 Yards

Panning right, you'll see the **Church and Castle of San Giorgio,** with its popular two-way viewpoint terrace, looking down over the port and out over the ocean. This is an easy option for a picnic with grand views. Boats back to Portofino depart from the harbor below this church. The Museo del Parco (described next) is also along this embankment.

Now look back toward town. A tidy grid of narrow cobbled streets angles gently uphill to the modern part of town, around Piazza della Libertà (with bus stop and taxi stand). These streets—where budget takeaway eateries and grocery stores are mixed in with swanky

Portofino's harborfront

Stop for a dip at Paraggi beach.

shops—are a good place to hunt for picnic fare. Up on the right is the striped church of San Martino, marking the well-manicured, enjoyable 30-minute trail to Paraggi beach.

Museo del Parco

For an artsy break, walk around the harbor to the right, where you can stroll around a park littered with 148 contemporary sculptures by mostly Italian artists, including a few top names (€5, open Wed-Mon 10:00-13:30 & 15:00-20:00 in summer; closed Tue, off-season, and in bad weather).

Hikes

The TIs in Portofino and Santa Margherita Ligure can outline your options. For even more detail, look at ParcoPortofino.com, a helpful website with sample itineraries. Here are two options easily doable from Portofino.

Lighthouse Hike: A paved stone path winds up and down to the lighthouse (*faro*) at the scenic point beyond the Church and Castle of San Giorgio. Start your climb on little Salita San Giorgio—it's tucked between the Delfino and Tripoli restaurants on the harborfront. Spend a few minutes enjoying the views on the church terrace (and if it's open, duck into the flower-bedecked cemetery behind the church). Rejoin the path signed al Faro to continue up. Walls and hedges block views at some points, but in the end, you'll be rewarded with the open sea—and a lounge/bar (open May-Sept, 25-minute walk). Consider popping into the medieval Castello Brown on the way up or down.

Paraggi Beach Hike: You can stroll the hilly pedestrian promenade through the trees from Portofino to Paraggi beach—if you're lucky, you might see a wild boar en route (30 minutes, path starts to the right of striped Divo Martino church just above the harborfront piazza, and ends at ritzy Paraggi beach, where bus #782 stops on its way back to Santa Margherita Ligure—though in peak season, the bus may be full and won't stop).

EATING IN PORTOFINO

Bring a picnic if you want to eat affordably in this beautiful village. Fancy restaurants ring the harbor, but the quality often doesn't match the high prices. I'd rather dine in Santa Margherita Ligure. There are a few glitzy cafés and bakeries in the back streets, but you won't find any bargains.

If you do eat in Portofino, **$$$$ Ristorante lo Stella,** just a few steps from the boat dock, has well-prepared dishes and portholes in the bathrooms (+39 0185 269 007). **$$$$ Taverna del Marinaio,** across the harbor, has a prime location to soak up the last of the day's sun, tables under arcades, and a small, cozy, classy interior (+39 0185 269 103). And **$$$$ Puny,** at the top of the harborfront square, is a famous splurge (reserve ahead, +39 0185 269 037, https://punyportofino.it). There are several *gelaterie,* including **Calata 32,** opposite the boat dock.

South of the Cinque Terre

South of the Cinque Terre is the nothing-special city of La Spezia, a handy transit hub with excellent train connections. And near La Spezia is a gem—the resort town of Porto Venere, worthy of a day trip from the Cinque Terre (by direct boat, or by train and bus via La Spezia).

Porto Venere

The enchanting village of Porto Venere (POR-toh VEH-neh-reh) hides just around the bay from La Spezia. Comparably scenic to the Cinque Terre towns—but with a bit of glitz and a darker history—Porto Venere clings to a rocky, fortress-crowned promontory. A rainbow of tall, skinny pastel facades rises from its inviting harborfront promenade.

Little Porto Venere is light on sights, but it's a breeze to reach by boat from the Cinque Terre and fun to explore: The higher you go, the better the views. Rather than the open sea, Porto Venere faces the beautiful Gulf of La Spezia—more romantically known as the Gulf of Poets—where Lord Byron was said to have gone for a hardy swim despite rough seas and local warnings to the contrary. (He survived…at least for a little while longer.) Scanning the bay, you'll see the outskirts of muscular La Spezia, the often-snow-covered peaks of the Apuan Alps, the resort town of Lerici, and—across a narrow strait—the rugged island of Palmaria.

GETTING TO PORTO VENERE

By Boat: Porto Venere is an easy day trip from the Cinque Terre towns by **boat** (late April-mid-Oct, 1.5 hours from Monterosso, €20 one-way, €37 day pass allows hopping on and off, +39 0187 732 987, see schedule at www.navigazionegolfodeipoeti.it).

By Train and Bus: The budget route to Porto Venere is by train to La Spezia and then by city **bus #P or #11 to Porto Venere.** The bus stop closest to the La Spezia Centrale train station is about a 15-minute walk away, on Via Nicolo Fieschi, the extension of Viale Garibaldi (see the "La Spezia" map in the next section for location—stops are marked "Fermata ATC"; 2/hour, 30 minutes, €2.50 each way; buy ticket at tobacco shop or newsstand in train station; www.atcesercizio.it). You could take the boat one way and the bus back (or vice versa), giving you a chance to explore La Spezia as well.

By Car: For **drivers,** parking is challenging. In peak season, shuttle buses connect the parking lot just outside Porto Venere to the harborside square. Otherwise, test your luck with the pay spots on the seaside.

Visiting Porto Venere

Tourist Information: The TI (Pro Loco Porto Venere) fills an old guard tower at the top of the main square (daily 10:00-12:00, also

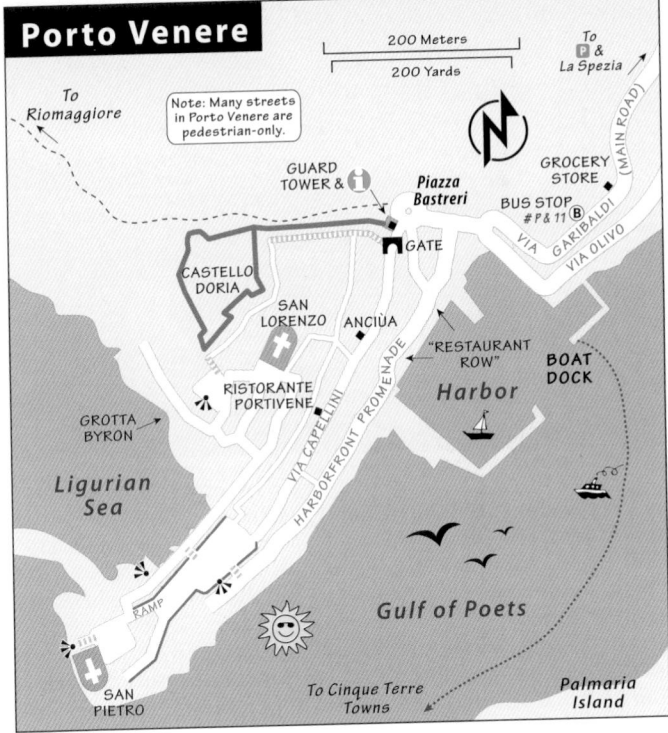

Porto Venere

200 Meters
200 Yards

To Riomaggiore

Note: Many streets in Porto Venere are pedestrian-only.

To P & La Spezia

GUARD TOWER & ℹ

Piazza Bastreri

GROCERY STORE

BUS STOP #P & 11 Ⓑ

GATE

VIA GARIBALDI (MAIN ROAD)

VIA OLIVO

CASTELLO DORIA

SAN LORENZO

ANCIÙA

"RESTAURANT ROW"

BOAT DOCK

Harbor

RISTORANTE PORTIVENE

VIA CAPELLINI

HARBORFRONT PROMENADE

GROTTA BYRON

Ligurian Sea

Gulf of Poets

RAMP

SAN PIETRO

To Cinque Terre Towns

Palmaria Island

Thu-Sun 15:00-17:00, shorter hours off-season, Piazza Bastreri 7, +39 0187 790 691, www.portovenere.com).

The town is essentially two streets deep: the harborfront promenade (Via Capellini), a block uphill. A complete loop around Porto Venere includes both of these streets and a moderately steep hike up to the town's two main churches and fortress for the views. You can see everything in just a few hours; add more time for lunch or lingering.

Along the **harborfront,** seafood restaurants enjoy a Technicolor backdrop and boat captains try to talk you into a 40-minute excursion around Palmaria and two other nearby islands. But all the action is

Lovely Porto Venere offers grand views to hikers and a harborfront promenade.

on **Via Capellini** (just through the big arch from the TI—or hike up any of the narrow stepped lanes from the harbor). Skinny and shaded, Via Capellini has a mix of restaurants, focaccia-and-pizza takeaway stands, local shops, and boutiques selling gourmet gifty edibles and gaudy beachwear.

At the west end of the promenade and Via Capellini, the town and its fortifications come to a point at the late-13th-century **Church of San Pietro,** with Gothic features and a black-and-white-striped interior typical of this region. Climb the stairs to the roof terrace for fine views in both directions (including the "Grotta Byron" sea cave).

More viewpoints line the walk from here up the stairs to the town's other big church, **San Lorenzo.** With a dark and brooding Romanesque interior, this church—like much of Porto Venere—was built by the Genovese to establish a strategic foothold at the entrance to the bay in the 12th century.

From in front of the church, more steps lead up to the town's fortress, **Castello Doria.** A hulking shell, it's not worth the money to go inside, but a hike up to the terrace out front is rewarded with striking panoramas.

From the castle, head back into town; to make this walk a loop,

Porto Venere's narrow lanes offer a mix of shops and restaurants.

bear left to follow the very steeply stepped lane that runs just inside the crenellated wall back down to the TI.

Hardy **hikers** enjoy the five-hour (or more) hike to Riomaggiore, the nearest Cinque Terre town. For more on hiking the Cinque Terre, see page 22.

EATING IN PORTO VENERE

On the harbor, take your pick of views and menus (seafood/pizza) for a meal along "Restaurant Row" in a memorable setting next to colorful bobbing boats.

For better values and more variety, stroll one block inland to Via Capellini. For a sit-down meal along here, try **$$ Ristorante Portivene,** serving local dishes with modern flair at reasonable prices (reservations smart, closed Mon, at #94, +39 0187 792 722). Better yet, browse the fun selection of takeaway shops (selling pizza slices, bruschetta, focaccia, and top-notch deli items) to put together a picnic to enjoy by the port. **$ Anciùa** (at #40) assembles *panini* to order with interesting ingredients; they also have fresh fried anchovies and other Ligurian street food.

La Spezia

While it's the next train stop south of the fanciful Cinque Terre, the working city of La Spezia (lah SPEH-tsee-ah; pop. 93,000) feels like "reality Italy." Useful as a transit point, La Spezia is slim on sights and has no beaches. You'll change trains here if traveling between the Cinque Terre and points farther south in Italy, and you'll see at least a bit of La Spezia if you use the bus to daytrip to Porto Venere—or if you arrive on one of the big cruise ships that funnel groups into the Cinque Terre.

ORIENTATION TO LA SPEZIA

Arrival in La Spezia: Get off at the La Spezia Centrale train station—not the suburban La Spezia Migliarina station, where some trains terminate. Along track 1 is a Cinque Terre National Park information desk, which sells park cards (see page 22) and acts as a TI (daily 8:00-19:00, shorter hours off-season, www.parconazionale5terre.it). You'll also find an office selling tickets for the Cinque Terre boats, a tobacco store, and a newsstand (handy if you need a ticket for the bus to Porto Venere). The city TI is a 10-minute walk away.

For **drivers** who want to leave a car in La Spezia then head to the Cinque Terre by train, the easiest parking is under the train station, at the modern Park Centro Stazione (enter from Via Fiume or Via Paleocapa, €30/day, www.mobpark.eu). There are cheaper lots a bus ride away.

Visiting La Spezia

The city center is a 10-minute walk downhill from the station, and the waterfront is another 10 minutes beyond that. Leave the station, turn left, and walk a long downhill block (on Via Pietro Paleocapa) to the big roundabout (Piazza Saint Bon). A nice pedestrian street starts on the other side of the roundabout, first called **Via Fiume** and, lower down, **Via del Prione.** You can continue on this street all the way to the harborfront gardens.

On your way you'll pass the **TI** at Via del Prione 228 (daily 9:00-12:30 and 15:00-19:00, shorter hours off-season, +39 0187 026 152, www.myspezia.it). The side streets leading off to the right are worth

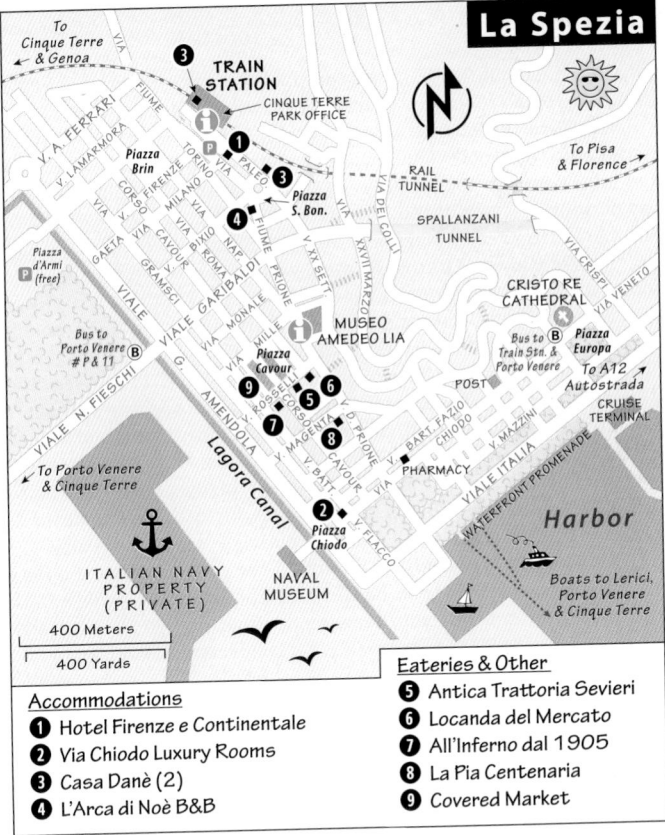

Accommodations

1. Hotel Firenze e Continentale
2. Via Chiodo Luxury Rooms
3. Casa Danè (2)
4. L'Arca di Noè B&B

Eateries & Other

5. Antica Trattoria Sevieri
6. Locanda del Mercato
7. All'Inferno dal 1905
8. La Pia Centenaria
9. Covered Market

exploring, such as Via Fratelli Rosselli, which leads to recommended restaurants and La Spezia's atmospheric covered market. Next to the TI is the nearly deserted **Museo Amedeo Lia,** a grab bag of Italian art and archaeology up to the 18th century, including some minor works by Venetian masters (€8, Tue-Sun 10:00-18:00, closed Mon, +39 0187-731-100, http://museolia.spezianet.it).

SLEEPING IN LA SPEZIA

Stay in the Cinque Terre if you can. La Spezia is a functional home base if there's no room elsewhere or if you've got a car to park.

$$ Hotel Firenze e Continentale, 100 yards from the train station, is a big, good-value, nicely modernized hotel with 70 rooms and lofty common spaces (RS%—request by email, air-con, elevator, pay parking—reserve ahead, Via Pietro Paleocapa 7, +39 0187 713 210, www.hotelfirenzecontinentale.it, info@hotelfirenzecontinentale.it).

$$ Via Chiodo Luxury Rooms, with nine elegant, bright-white rooms on the second floor of a large downtown building, is a soothing retreat near the harbor and close to the public gardens—though if you're coming from the train station, you'll probably want a taxi (air-con, elevator, no parking, Via Chiodo 13, +39 0187 22 607, see "Via Chiodo Luxury Rooms" at www.costaestate.it, info@costaestate.it).

$$ Casa Danè offers 10 chic rooms with comfy linens and orange trees outside the door, plus 20 more rooms inside the train station. Some rooms overlook the tracks, but good windows reduce the noise (RS%—use code "RICK2023," family rooms, air-con, Via Paleocapa 4, +39 338 535 3103, www.casadane.it, reception@casadane.it, Paolo).

$ L'Arca di Noè B&B, at the top of the pedestrian zone a five-minute walk from the station, has three bright, artsy, affordable rooms, all with private bath (air-con, homey communal kitchen, Via Fiume 39, mobile +39 320 485 2434, montialex74@gmail.com, Alessandra).

EATING IN LA SPEZIA

These eateries are within a 10-minute walk of the train station.

$$$ Antica Trattoria Sevieri is an elegant place across from the covered market, featuring fresh fish and superb seafood pastas and risotto (Mon-Sat 12:00-15:00 & 19:00-24:00, closed Sun, Via della Canonica 13, +39 0187 751 1776).

$$ Locanda del Mercato has white tablecloths, formal service, and Ligurian specialties that you can savor inside or out (Wed-Mon 11:30-15:30 & 18:30-23:30, closed Tue, Via Fratelli Rosselli 88, +39 0187 732 651).

$ All'Inferno dal 1905, a small, busy, less-expensive restaurant with a laid-back atmosphere, serves traditional chickpea soup (*mesciua*), linguine with mussels, and homemade pesto. Look for the red door in the narrow cross-street of Piazza Cavour (Mon-Sat 12:15-14:30 & 19:30-22:30, closed Sun, +39 0187 29458, Via L. Costa 3).

$ La Pia Centenaria draws local crowds to its takeaway counter for its specialty—*farinata* (€2-5 chickpea pancakes, eaten plain or with savory toppings). They also sell focaccia and pizza by the slice and have a separate, simple sit-down section with table service (Mon-Sat 11:00-15:00 & 17:00-22:00, closed Sun, Via Magenta 12, +39 0187 739 999, www.lapia.it).

LA SPEZIA CONNECTIONS

Trains leave at least twice hourly for the **Cinque Terre towns** (direction: Levanto or Sestri Levante). A few express trains (headed to Genoa or Milan) stop only at Monterosso. Other connections from La Spezia include **Pisa** (at least hourly, 50-80 minutes), **Florence** (5/day direct, 2.5 hours, or nearly hourly with change in Pisa), **Rome** (8/day direct, 3-4 hours, more with change in Pisa), **Milan** (about every 2 hours direct, 3.5 hours), and **Venice** (6 hours, change in Milan or Florence).

It's also possible to go by **boat** to the Cinque Terre, Porto Venere, and outer islands from La Spezia (www.navigazionegolfodeipoeti.it). The boat office in the train station sells tickets.

Practicalities

HELPFUL HINTS

Travel Tips

Travel Advisories: Before traveling, check updated health and safety conditions, including restrictions for your destination, on the travel pages of the US State Department (www.travel.state.gov) and Centers for Disease Control and Prevention (www.cdc.gov/travel).

Hurdling the Language Barrier: Many Italians—especially those in the tourist trade and in big cities—speak English. Still, you'll get better treatment if you learn and use Italian pleasantries. Italians have an endearing habit of talking to you even if they know you don't speak their language—and yet, thanks to gestures and thoughtfully simplified words, it somehow works. Don't stop them to tell them you don't understand every word—just go along for the ride. For a list of survival phrases, see page 177.

Time Zones: Italy is six/nine hours ahead of the East/West Coasts of the US. For a handy time converter, use the world clock app on your phone or download one (see www.timeanddate.com).

Business Hours: Most businesses are open Monday through Saturday 9:00 to 13:00 and from 15:30-16:00 to 19:00-19:30. Many shops stay open through lunch or later into the evening, especially larger stores in tourist areas. Shops in small towns and villages are more likely to close during lunch. Stores are usually closed on Sunday, and often on Monday. Many shops close for a couple of weeks around August 15.

Watt's Up: Europe's electrical system is 220 volts, instead of North America's 110 volts. Most electronics (laptops, phones, cameras) and appliances (newer hair dryers, CPAP machines) convert

Learning some Italian will endear you to locals.

Use an ATM attached to a bank for lower fees.

PRACTICALITIES

Helpful Websites

Italian Tourist Information: Italia.it

Cinque Terre Tourist Information: CinqueTerre.it

Cinque Terre National Park: ParcoNazionale5terre.it

Passports and Red Tape: Travel.state.gov

Cheap Flights: Kayak.com (international flights), SkyScanner.com (flights within Europe)

Airplane Carry-on Restrictions: TSA.gov

European Train Schedules: Bahn.com

General Travel Tips: RickSteves.com (train travel, rail passes, car rental, travel insurance, packing lists, and much more)

automatically, so you won't need a converter, but you will need an adapter plug with two round prongs, sold inexpensively at travel stores in the US.

Safety and Emergencies

Emergency and Medical Help: For any emergency service—ambulance, police, or fire—call **112** from a mobile phone or landline. If you get sick, do as the locals do and go to a pharmacist for advice. Or ask at your hotel for help—they'll know the nearest medical and emergency services.

Theft or Loss: Petty theft is common around heavily touristed areas. With sweet-talking con artists meeting you at the station and well-dressed pickpockets on buses, tourists face a gauntlet of rip-offs. Pickpockets don't want to hurt you—they usually just want your money and gadgets. Green or sloppy tourists are prone to scams. Thieves strike when you're distracted. Don't trust overly kind strangers. Keep nothing important in your pockets, and be especially careful with expensive cell phones.

To replace a **passport,** you'll need to go in person to an embassy or consulate. **US** embassy in Rome—+39 06 46741, passport and nonemergency consular services, by appointment only (Via Vittorio Veneto 121). Consulates in Milan—+39 02 290 351 (Via Principe Amedeo 2/10); Florence—+39 055 266 951 (Lungarno Vespucci 38); and Naples—+39 081 583 8111 (Piazza della Repubblica). For all, see http://it.usembassy.

gov. **Canadian** embassy in Rome—+39 06 854 442 911 (Via Zara 30); Milan—+39 02 626 94238 (Piazza Cavour 3). For both, see www.italy. gc.ca. After-hours emergency in Ottawa +1 613 996 8885.

   If your credit and debit cards disappear, cancel and replace them, and report the loss immediately (with a mobile phone, call these 24-hour US numbers: Visa—+1 303 967 1096, MasterCard—+1 636 722 7111, and American Express—+1 336 393 1111). For more information, see RickSteves.com/help.

MONEY

Italy uses the euro currency: 1 euro (€) = about $1.10. To convert prices in euros to dollars, add about 10 percent: €20 = about $22, €50 = about $55. Check www.oanda.com for the latest exchange rates.

   You'll use your **credit card** for purchases both big (hotels, advance tickets) and small (little shops, food stands). A "tap-to-pay" or "contactless" card is the most widely accepted and simplest to use. Get comfortable using contactless pay options. Check to see if you already have—or can get—a tap-to-pay version of your credit card (look on the card for the tap-to-pay symbol—four curvy lines). Make sure you know the numeric, four-digit PIN for each of your cards, both debit and credit. Request it if you don't have one, as it may be required for some purchases.

   Use a **debit card** at ATMs (called a *bancomat*) to withdraw a small amount of local cash. While most transactions are by card these days, cash can help you out of a jam if your card randomly doesn't work, and can be useful to pay for things like tips and local guides. Keep your cards and cash safe in a **money belt.**

   At self-service payment machines (such as transit-ticket kiosks), US cards may not work. In this case, look for a cashier who can process your card manually—or pay in cash.

VAT and Customs

The Cinque Terre has limited options for shoppers, such as tacky (if fun) beach trinkets and T-shirts. Some of the towns have higher-quality art boutiques. But in general, the Cinque Terre's best souvenirs are edible, such as a jar of pesto, dried *trofie* pasta to go with it, olive oil, the sweet *sciacchetrà* dessert wine, and items with lemon flavors or scents.

Tipping

Tipping in Italy isn't as automatic and generous as it is in the US.

Restaurants: In Italy, a service charge (*servizio*) is usually built in to your check (look at the bill carefully). If it is included, there's no need to leave an extra tip. If it's not included, it's common to leave about €1 per person (a bit more at finer restaurants) or to round up the bill. If paying with a credit card, be prepared to tip separately with cash or coins; credit card receipts don't often have a tip line.

Taxis: For a typical ride, round up your fare a bit (for instance, if the fare is €4.50, pay €5).

Services: In general, if someone in the tourism or service industry does a super job for you, a small tip of a euro or two is appropriate...but not required.

Getting a VAT Refund: If you purchase more than €155 worth of goods at a single store, you may be eligible to get a refund of the 22 percent Value-Added Tax (VAT). Get more details from the merchant or see RickSteves.com/vat.

Customs for American Shoppers: You can take home $800 worth of items per person duty-free, once every 31 days. You can bring in one liter of alcohol duty-free. For details on allowable goods, customs rules, and duty rates, visit Help.cbp.gov.

SLEEPING

My sleeping recommendations run the gamut, from dorm beds to luxurious rooms with all of the comforts. I like places that are clean, central, reasonably priced, friendly, small enough to have a hands-on owner or manager, and run with a respect for Italian traditions. Most of my recommendations fall short of perfection. But if I can find a place with most of these features, it's a keeper.

Book your accommodations as soon as your itinerary is set, especially if you want to stay at one of my top listings or if you'll be traveling during busy times. See the sidebar later for a list of major holidays and festivals in the Cinque Terre.

Sleep Code

Dollar signs reflect average rates for a standard double room with breakfast in high season.

$$$$	**Splurge:** Most rooms over €170
$$$	**Pricier:** €130-170
$$	**Moderate:** €90-130
$	**Budget:** €50-90
¢	**Backpacker:** Under €50
RS%	**Rick Steves discount**

Unless otherwise noted, credit cards are accepted, hotel staff speak basic English, and free Wi-Fi is available. If the listing includes RS%, request a Rick Steves discount.

Part of the pleasure of planning a trip to the Cinque Terre is settling on which town to stay in.

Vernazza, the salty essence of the Cinque Terre, is my top choice for a home base. Its summer opera series has beefed up its nightlife. But if you think too many people have my book, you'll get fewer crowds and better value for your money in other towns.

Monterosso is a good choice for sun-worshipping beach lovers, those who prefer the ease of a real hotel, and those interested in youthful nightlife.

Manarola, charming and not overrun, draws serious hikers and sophisticated Europeans. The town has a good range of professional-feeling small accommodations (and a youth hostel), but fewer dining and evening options.

Riomaggiore, the second-largest Cinque Terre town, has the cheapest beds and rivals Monterosso for nightlife.

Corniglia, on a hilltop (no harbor), attracts hermits, anarchists, wine lovers, and mountain goats. It also has a hostel.

Many accommodations in the Cinque Terre (especially in Vernazza) are **private rooms for rent** (*affittacamere*). The typical offer is a nicely done-up bedroom with private bath or a comfortable apartment with a small kitchen. You get a key and come and go as you like, rarely seeing your landlord, who lives elsewhere and may manage

five or ten such rooms. Expect thin walls (pack earplugs). Plan on paying cash. If you must cancel an *affittacamere* reservation, do it as early as possible—since people renting rooms usually don't take deposits, they lose money if you don't show up.

Breakfast: Breakfast is not included at most *affittacamere* and other simple accommodations. Locals don't make much of breakfast anyway: The basic, very Italian approach is to drop by a neighborhood bar for a cappuccino and a *cornetto* (croissant) or a piece of focaccia. Some pricier places include breakfast, but this often consists of a few paltry items (packaged croissants, yogurt, instant coffee) in a mini-fridge in your room.

Air-Conditioning: While air-conditioning is essential in the summer elsewhere in Italy, in the breezy Cinque Terre you can generally manage fine without it.

Near the Cinque Terre

Riviera towns typically have modern hotels with the usual amenities. The hotels aren't necessarily cheaper than the Cinque Terre, but they are more likely to have space. High season is roughly May through September, peaking in July and August. Some hotels close in winter.

EATING

Hanging out at a seaview restaurant while sampling local treats could become one of your favorite Cinque Terre memories.

Fresh anchovies (*acciughe;* ah-CHOO-gay)—ideally served the day they're caught—are a staple protein here. If you've always hated preserved anchovies (the slimy, salty kind), try them fresh here. These little fish are prepared in a dizzying variety of ways: marinated, salted, drenched in lemon juice, butterflied and deep-fried (sometimes with a tasty garlic/vinegar sauce called *giada*), and so on. A favorite way to prepare fresh anchovies is baked in a casserole, layered whole with potatoes, tomatoes, white wine, oil, and herbs (look on menus for *tegame alla vernazzana*).

Seafood is plentiful. You'll often see *muscoli ripieni* (stuffed mussels) on menus. And, while antipasto means cheese and salami in Tuscany, here you'll get *antipasti frutti di mare* (or simply *antipasti misti*): a plate of mixed "fruits of the sea." Many restaurants are proud of their *frutti di mare*—it's how they show off—and it's a fine way to start a meal. For two diners, splitting one of these and a pasta dish can be plenty.

This region is the birthplace of pesto. Basil, which loves the temperate Ligurian climate, is ground with cheese (half *parmigiano* and half *pecorino*), garlic, olive oil, and pine nuts, and then poured over pasta. You'll see it on gnocchi or on pasta designed specifically for pesto to cling to: *trenette* (ruffled on one side) or *trofie* (short, dense twists). Many also like pesto lasagna, made with white sauce.

Pansotti are ravioli with ricotta and a mixture of greens, often served with a walnut sauce (*salsa di noci*)...delightful and filling.

Focaccia—pillowy, flat, salty, olive-oily bread—also originates here in Liguria. The baker roughs up the dough with finger holes, sprinkles it with salt water, then bakes it. Focaccia comes plain or with onions, sage, or olives, and is a local favorite for a snack on the beach. Bakeries sell it in rounds or slices by weight (a portion is about 100 grams, or *un etto*).

Farinata, a humble flatbread snack sold at pizza and focaccia places, is made from chickpea flour, water, oil, and pepper and baked on a copper tray in a wood-burning stove. It's dense, filling, and less flavorful than focaccia.

The region also loves its locally grown lemons. Lemon liqueur here is called *limoncino*—it's the same as what's called *limoncello* in southern Italy.

Vino delle Cinque Terre, while not one of Italy's top wines, flows cheap and easy throughout the region. It's white—crisp, refreshing, and great with seafood. It's defined as a blend, predominantly using the bosco grape, grown only here. Local wine has become more sophisticated and appreciated, and plenty of wine bars offer tasting experiences.

Restaurant Code

Dollar signs reflect the cost of a typical main course.

$$$$ **Splurge:** Most main courses over €25
$$$ **Pricier:** €20-25
$$ **Moderate:** €15-20
$ **Budget:** Under €15

Pizza by the slice and other takeaway food is **$**; a basic trattoria or sit-down pizzeria is **$$**; a casual but more upscale restaurant is **$$$**; and a swanky splurge is **$$$$**.

A sweet but potent dessert wine, the local *sciacchetrà* (shah-keh-TRAH) is worth a try (18 percent alcohol, often served with dunkable cookies). Like the German *Eiswein,* it's sweet because it's made from near-raisins; 10 kilos of grapes make only 1.5 liters of *sciacchetrà.* The word means roughly "crush and pull"—crush lots of grapes, pull out the best wine.

STAYING CONNECTED

Making International Calls

From a Mobile Phone: Phone numbers in this book are presented exactly as you would dial them from a US mobile phone. For international access, press and hold 0 (zero) to get a + sign, then dial the country code (39 for Italy) and phone number.

From a US Landline to Europe: Replace + with 011 (US/Canada access code), then dial the country code (39 for Italy) and phone number.

From a European Landline to the US or Europe: Replace + with 00 (Europe access code), then dial the country code (39 for Italy, 1 for the US) and phone number. For more phoning help, see HowToCallAbroad.com.

Using Your Phone in Europe

Sign up for an international plan. To stay connected at a lower cost, sign up for an international service plan through your carrier. Most

Events in the Cinque Terre

Use this list to find and join a festival—or to avoid crowds. For more festival information and to confirm dates, check LaMiaLiguria.it. Food festivals in particular are subject to change.

Easter and Easter Monday	**Popular time to visit the Cinque Terre.** As it's extremely crowded, book long in advance.
April 25	**Italian Liberation Day.** Avoid this day, as locals literally shut down the trails.
May 1	**Labor Day.** Day-trippers pack the five towns.
May (3rd Sunday)	**Monterosso: Lemon Festival**
June (3rd Sunday)	**Monterosso: Anchovy Festival**
June 23	**Monterosso and Vernazza: Feast of Corpus Domini** (procession on carpet of flowers)
June 24	**Riomaggiore and Monterosso: Feast day of St. John the Baptist** (procession and fireworks, floating candles on the sea; big fire on Monterosso's old-town beach the day before)
June 29	**Corniglia: Feast day of Sts. Peter and Paul**
July 20	**Vernazza: Feast day of patron St. Margaret,** with fireworks
Aug (1st Sunday)	**Vernazza: Feast of Nostra Signora di Reggio** (hike up to Madonna di Reggio sanctuary for food and church procession)
Aug 10	**Manarola: Feast day of patron St. Lawrence**
Aug 15	**Feast of the Assumption** (Ferragosto)
Sept 8	**Monterosso: Feast of Madonna di Fegina** (luminarias and procession up to hilltop sanctuary)

providers offer a simple bundle that includes calling, messaging, and data.

Use free Wi-Fi whenever possible. Unless you have an unlimited-data plan, save most of your online tasks for Wi-Fi. Most accommodations in Europe offer free Wi-Fi, and many cafés offer hotspots for customers. You may also find Wi-Fi at TIs, city squares, major museums, public-transit hubs, airports, and aboard trains and buses.

Minimize use of your cellular network. Even with an international data plan, wait until you're on Wi-Fi to Skype or FaceTime, download apps, stream videos, or do other megabyte-greedy tasks. Using a navigation app such as Google Maps over a cellular network can require lots of data, so download maps when you're on Wi-Fi, then use the app offline.

Use Wi-Fi calling and messaging apps. Skype, WhatsApp, FaceTime, and Google Meet are great for making free or low-cost calls or sending texts over Wi-Fi worldwide.

RESOURCES FROM RICK STEVES

Begin your trip at RickSteves.com: This book is just one of many in my series on European travel. I also produce a public television series, *Rick Steves' Europe,* and a public radio show, *Travel with Rick Steves.* My mobile-friendly website is *the* place to explore Europe in preparation for your trip. You'll find thousands of fun articles, videos, and radio interviews; a wealth of money-saving tips; travel news dispatches; a video library of travel talks; my travel blog; our latest guidebook updates (RickSteves.com/update); and the free Rick Steves Audio Europe app with audio tours of Europe's top sights. You can also follow me on Facebook, Instagram, and Twitter.

Packing Checklist

Clothing

- ❏ 5 shirts: long- & short-sleeve
- ❏ 2 pairs pants (or skirts/capris)
- ❏ 1 pair shorts
- ❏ 5 pairs underwear & socks
- ❏ 1 pair walking shoes
- ❏ Sweater or warm layer
- ❏ Rainproof jacket with hood
- ❏ Tie, scarf, belt, and/or hat
- ❏ Swimsuit
- ❏ Sleepwear/loungewear

Money

- ❏ Debit card(s)
- ❏ Credit card(s)
- ❏ Hard cash (US $100-200)
- ❏ Money belt

Documents

- ❏ Passport
- ❏ Other required ID: Vaccine card/Covid test, entry visa, etc.
- ❏ Driver's license, student ID, hostel card, etc.
- ❏ Tickets & confirmations: flights, hotels, trains, rail pass, car rental, sight entries
- ❏ Photocopies of important documents
- ❏ Insurance details
- ❏ Guidebooks & maps
- ❏ Extra passport photos
- ❏ Notepad & pen
- ❏ Journal

Toiletries

- ❏ Soap, shampoo, toothbrush, toothpaste, floss, deodorant, sunscreen, brush/comb, etc.
- ❏ Medicines & vitamins
- ❏ First-aid kit
- ❏ Glasses/contacts/sunglasses
- ❏ Face masks & hand sanitizer
- ❏ Sewing kit
- ❏ Packet of tissues (for WC)
- ❏ Earplugs

Electronics

- ❏ Mobile phone
- ❏ Camera & related gear
- ❏ Tablet/ebook reader/laptop
- ❏ Headphones/earbuds
- ❏ Chargers & batteries
- ❏ Plug adapters

Miscellaneous

- ❏ Daypack
- ❏ Sealable plastic baggies
- ❏ Laundry supplies
- ❏ Small umbrella
- ❏ Travel alarm/watch

Optional Extras

- ❏ Second pair of shoes
- ❏ Travel hairdryer
- ❏ Disinfecting wipes
- ❏ Water bottle
- ❏ Fold-up tote bag
- ❏ Small flashlight & binoculars
- ❏ Small towel or washcloth
- ❏ Tiny lock

Italian Survival Phrases

Hello. (informal)	Ciao.	chow
Good day.	Buongiorno.	bwohn-**jor**-noh
Do you speak English?	Parla inglese?	**par**-lah een-**gleh**-zay
Yes. / No.	Sì. / No.	see / noh
I (don't) understand.	(Non) capisco.	(nohn) kah-**pees**-koh
Please.	Per favore.	pehr fah-**voh**-ray
Thank you.	Grazie.	**graht**-see-ay
You're welcome.	Prego.	**preh**-go
I'm sorry.	Mi dispiace.	mee dee-spee-**ah**-chay
Excuse me.	Mi scusi.	mee **skoo**-zee
No problem.	*Non c'è problema.*	nohn cheh proh-**bleh**-mah
Goodbye.	Arrivederci.	ah-ree-veh-**dehr**-chee
one / two / three	uno / due / tre	**oo**-noh / **doo**-ay / tray
How much is it?	Quanto costa?	**kwahn**-toh **koh**-stah
I'd like / We'd like...	Vorrei / Vorremmo...	voh-**reh**-ee / voh-**reh**-moh
...a room.	...una camera.	**oo**-nah **kah**-meh-rah
...a ticket to _____.	...un biglietto per _____.	oon beel-**yeh**-toh pehr _____
Where is...?	Dov'è...?	doh-**veh**
...the train station	...la stazione	lah staht-see-**oh**-nay
...tourist information	...informazioni turisti	een-for-maht-see-**oh**-nee too-**ree**-stee
...the bathroom	...il bagno	eel **bahn**-yoh
men / women	uomini, signori / donne, signore	**woh**-mee-nee, seen-**yoh**-ree / **doh**-nay, seen-**yoh**-ray
left / right / straight	sinistra / destra / sempre dritto	see-**nee**-strah / **deh**-strah / **sehm**-pray **dree**-toh
What time does this open / close?	A che ora apre / chiude?	ah kay **oh**-rah **ah**-pray / kee-**oo**-day
now / soon / later	adesso / presto / tardi	ah-**deh**-soh / **preh**-stoh / **tar**-dee
today / tomorrow	oggi / domani	**oh**-jee / doh-**mah**-nee

In an Italian Restaurant

I'd like / We'd like...	Vorrei / Vorremmo... voh-**reh**-ee / voh-**reh**-moh
...to reserve a table for one / two.	...prenotare un tavolo per uno / due. preh-noh-**tah**-ray oon **tah**-voh-loh pehr **oo**-noh / **doo**-ay
...the menu (in English).	...il menù (in inglese). eel meh-**noo** (een een-**gleh**-zay)
service (not) included	servizio (non) compreso sehr-**veet**-see-oh (nohn) kohm-**pray**-zoh
cover charge	pane e coperto **pah**-nay ay koh-**pehr**-toh
to go	da portar via dah **por**-tar **vee**-ah
with / without	con / senza kohn / **sehnt**-sah
and / or	e / o ay / oh
breakfast / lunch / dinner	colazione / pranzo / cena koh-laht-zee-**oh**-nay / **prahn**-zoh / **chay**-nah
menu (of the day)	menù (d el giorno) meh-**noo** (dehl **jor**-noh)
specialty of the house	specialità della casa speh-chah-lee-**tah deh**-lah **kah**-zah
sandwich	panino pah-**nee**-noh
soup / salad	zuppa / insalata **tsoo**-pah / een-sah-**lah**-tah
meat / chicken	carne / pollo **kar**-nay / **poh**-loh
fish / seafood	pesce / frutti di mare **peh**-shay / **froo**-tee dee **mah**-ray
fruit / vegetables	frutta / verdure **froo**-tah / vehr-**doo**-ray
dessert	dolce **dohl**-chay
tap water	acqua del rubinetto **ah**-kwah dehl roo-bee-**neh**-toh
coffee / tea	caffè / tè kah-**feh** / teh
wine / beer	vino / birra **vee**-noh / **bee**-rah
red / white	rosso / bianco **roh**-soh / bee-**ahn**-koh
glass / bottle	bicchiere / bottiglia bee-kee-**eh**-ray / boh-**teel**-yah
The bill, please.	Il conto, per favore. eel **kohn**-toh pehr fah-**voh**-ray
Do you accept credit cards?	Accettate carte di credito? ah-cheh-**tah**-tay **kar**-tay dee **kreh**-dee-toh
Delicious!	Delizioso! day-leet-see-**oh**-zoh

For more user-friendly Italian phrases, check out *Rick Steves Italian Phrase Book* or *Rick Steves French, Italian, & German Phrase Book*.

INDEX

Start your trip at

Explore Europe

At ricksteves.com you can browse through thousands of articles, videos, photos and radio interviews, plus find a wealth of money-saving travel tips for planning your dream trip. And with our mobile-friendly website, you can easily access all this great travel information anywhere you go.

TV Shows

Preview the places you'll visit by watching entire half-hour episodes of *Rick Steves' Europe* (choose from all 100 shows) on-demand, for free.

ricksteves.com

your travel dreams into affordable reality

Radio Interviews

Enjoy ready access to Rick's vast library of radio interviews covering travel tips and cultural insights that relate specifically to your Europe travel plans.

Travel Forums

Learn, ask, share! Our online community of savvy travelers is a great resource for first-time travelers to Europe, as well as seasoned pros.

Travel News

Subscribe to our free Travel News e-newsletter, and get monthly updates from Rick on what's happening in Europe.

Classroom Europe®

Check out our free resource for educators with 500 short video clips from the *Rick Steves' Europe* TV show.

Audio Europe™

Rick Steves AUDIO EUROPE

Rick's Free Travel App

Get your FREE Rick Steves Audio Europe™ app to enjoy...

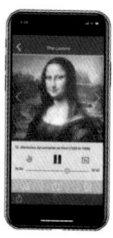

- Dozens of self-guided tours of Europe's top museums, sights and historic walks
- Hundreds of tracks filled with cultural insights and sightseeing tips from Rick's radio interviews
- All organized into handy geographic playlists
- For Apple and Android

With Rick whispering in your ear, Europe gets even better.

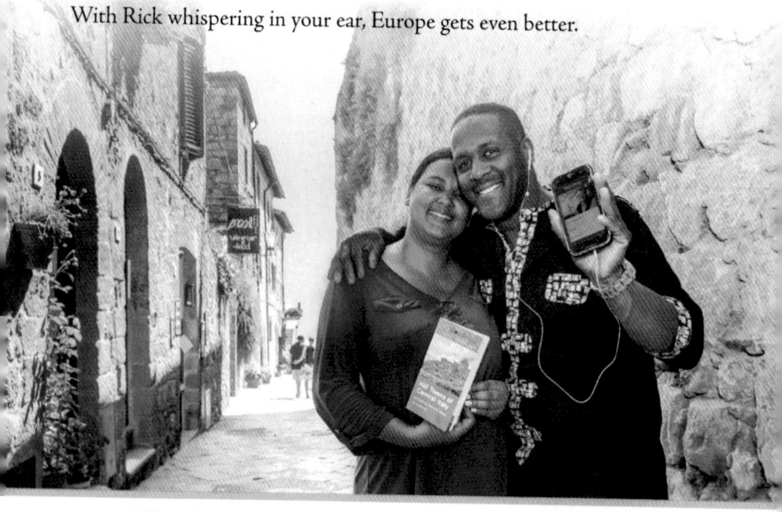

Find out more at ricksteves.com

Pack Light and Right

Gear up for your next adventure at ricksteves.com

Light Luggage

Pack light and right with Rick Steves' affordable, custom-designed rolling carry-on bags, backpacks, day packs and shoulder bags.

Accessories

From packing cubes to moneybelts and beyond, Rick has personally selected the travel goodies that will help your trip go smoother.

Shop at ricksteves.com

Rick Steves has

Experience maximum Europe

Save time and energy

This guidebook is your independent-travel toolkit. But for all it delivers, it's still up to you to devote the time and energy it takes to manage the preparation and logistics that are essential for a happy trip. If that's a hassle, there's a solution.

Rick Steves Tours

A Rick Steves tour takes you to Europe's most interesting places with great guides and small groups.

great tours, too!

with minimum stress

We follow Rick's favorite itineraries, ride in comfy buses, stay in family-run hotels, and bring you intimately close to the Europe you've traveled so far to see. Most importantly, we take away the logistical headaches so you can focus on the fun.

Join the fun

This year we'll take thousands of free-spirited travelers—nearly half of them repeat customers—along with us on four dozen different itineraries, from Ireland to Italy to Athens. Is a Rick Steves tour the right fit for your travel dreams? Find out at ricksteves.com, where you can check seat availability and sign up.

Europe is best experienced with happy travel partners. We hope you can join us.

See our itineraries at ricksteves.com

A Guide for Every Trip

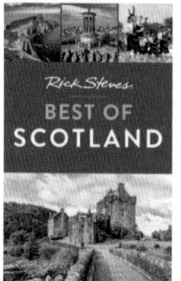

BEST OF GUIDES
Full-color guides in an easy-to-scan format, focusing on top sights and experiences in popular destinations

Best of England
Best of Europe
Best of France
Best of Germany

Best of Ireland
Best of Italy
Best of Scotland
Best of Spain

COMPREHENSIVE GUIDES
City, country, and regional guides printed on Bible-thin paper. Packed with detailed coverage for a multi-week trip exploring iconic sights and more

Amsterdam &
  the Netherlands
Barcelona
Belgium: Bruges, Brussels,
  Antwerp & Ghent
Berlin
Budapest
Croatia & Slovenia
Eastern Europe
England
Florence & Tuscany
France
Germany
Great Britain
Greece: Athens &
  the Peloponnese
Iceland

Ireland
Istanbul
Italy
London
Paris
Portugal
Prague & the Czech Republic
Provence & the French
  Riviera
Rome
Scandinavia
Scotland
Sicily
Spain
Switzerland
Venice
Vienna, Salzburg & Tirol

Many guides are available as ebooks.

POCKET GUIDES
Compact guides for shorter city trips

SNAPSHOT GUIDES
Focused single-destination coverage

CRUISE PORTS GUIDES
Reference for cruise ports of call

TRAVEL SKILLS & CULTURE
Greater information and insight

PHRASE BOOKS & DICTIONARIES

PLANNING MAPS

PHOTO CREDITS

Front Cover: Vernazza © Marco Arduino, Sime, eStock Photo

Title Page: Riomaggiore © Dominic Arizona Bonuccelli

Additional Photography: Dominic Arizona Bonuccelli, Orin Dubrow, Cameron Hewitt, Heather Lawless, Rick Steves, Ragen Van Sewell. Photos are used by permission and are the property of the original copyright owners.

Avalon Travel
Hachette Book Group
1700 Fourth Street
Berkeley, CA 94710

Printed in China by RR Donnelley
Third Edition. First printing October 2023

ISBN: 978-1-64171-567-6

For the latest on Rick's talks, guidebooks, tours, public television series, and public radio show, contact Rick Steves' Europe, 130 Fourth Avenue North, Edmonds, WA 98020, +1 425 771 8303, RickSteves.com, rick@ricksteves.com.

Rick Steves' Europe
Managing Editor: Jennifer Madison Davis
Assistant Managing Editor: Cathy Lu
Editors: Glenn Eriksen, Suzanne Kotz, Rosie Leutzinger, Teresa Nemeth, Jessica Shaw, Carrie Shepherd, Chelsea Wing
Graphic Content Director: Sandra Hundacker
Maps & Graphics: Orin Dubrow, David C. Hoerlein, Lauren Mills, Mary Rostad

Avalon Travel
Senior Editor and Series Manager: Madhu Prasher
Associate Managing Editors: Jamie Andrade, Sierra Machado
Copy Editor: Jenny Malnick
Proofreader: Kelly Lydick
Indexer: Claire Splan
Production & Typesetting: Christine DeLorenzo
Cover Design: Kimberly Glyder Design
Interior Design: Darren Alessi
Maps & Graphics: Kat Bennett

Let's Keep on Travelin'

Your trip doesn't need to end.

Follow Rick on social media!